Praise for *All That's Good*

When the topic of discernment arises, I get nervous. Maybe you do, too. Many of us have been on the receiving end of the well-intended comments of others, offered in the name of godly discernment. With the Bible as her steady guide, Hannah Anderson points us toward good definitions and good practices to help us obey the command to be people who know how to discern rightly. I'm so grateful for this clarifying book.

JEN WILKIN
Author and Bible teacher

Few authors capture the nuances of Christian wisdom and avoid reducing it to the "do's and don'ts of life" or "the five steps to sound decision-making." Yet in *All That's Good*, Hannah Anderson skillfully captures wisdom's many sides, delivering a thoughtful, informed, and accessible approach to the *art of discernment* for all Christians. By grounding her approach in God's good creation, Anderson calls readers to reconsider how God is at work in His world, how we experience the world around us, and especially *how we think* as we journey through life with God. For all who desire to cultivate virtue and grow in wisdom and discernment, move *All That's Good* to the top of your reading list. As both professor and pastor, I strongly recommend it.

BENJAMIN T. QUINN
Assistant Prof., Southeastern Baptist Theological Seminary
Pastor, Holly Grove Baptist Church

All That's Good urges us to grow in true discernment by developing a taste for God's goodness. Weaving nostalgic storytelling with wisdom and soul, Hannah beckons us to deep, biblical thinking. Readers will walk away looking for God's pure, lovely, redemptive, restoring character in the world around them. This is a timely book on an always relevant topic.

EMILY JENSEN AND LAURA WIFLER
Cofounders of Risen Motherhood

All That's Good has arrived at just the right moment. In an age of tribalism and "fake news," it's more important than ever that Christians develop their discernment skills in order to follow Christ well in spite of the challenges of our current cultural moment. Hannah illuminates eternal truths in an accessible manner that all Christians will walk away from this book with tools to navigate this present age as better neighbors, citizens, and disciples.

KATHRYN FREEMAN
Director of Public Policy, Texas Baptist Christian Life Commission

Once again, Hannah Anderson has written a book that not only points readers toward the good, the true, and the beautiful, but *is* all of these things as well. This book recovers life-giving, joy-generating applications of the Christian faith that have been lost for generations to the spirits of fear and enmity that have come to define the relationship of many believers to God's good world. Anderson's reminder to "taste and see" the goodness of God all around us is a welcome invitation for us all.

KAREN SWALLOW PRIOR
Author of *On Reading Well: Finding the Good Life through Great Books* and *Fierce Convictions: The Extraordinary Life of Hannah More—Poet, Reformer, Abolitionist*

Hannah Anderson has long been a source of wisdom and insight into the spiritual nature of the public and the public nature of the spiritual. She captures the truth about things we all see, but can hardly explain. In *All That's Good*, Hannah does it again, refusing the false public/private dichotomy that starves our public life and splits our souls in half. Reading this book will help you bring your whole self to the public, discerning what is good and what is not, and partnering with God to see His goodness become even more realized in the world. What a soul-nourishing read Hannah has provided for us in these pages.

MICHAEL WEAR
Author of *Reclaiming Hope: Lessons Learned in the Obama White House About the Future of Faith in America*

I've always seen discernment as a basically negative thing: make sure you don't embrace something bad. Hannah Anderson has convinced me that it is a positive thing: make sure you do embrace what is good. This book, like the biblical text it centers on, is good, true, honorable, excellent, and praiseworthy. Buy it, read it, and think about such things!

ANDREW WILSON
Teaching Pastor at King's Church London

Hannah Anderson presents a beautiful and needed guide for finding the good that's often hidden within the world's brokenness. In *All That's Good,* Hannah's signature storytelling revives the lost art of discernment and inspires us to hunt for His goodness in all the nooks and crannies of life. From family relations to community involvement to political discourse, *All That's Good* trains us to sort through the constant barrage of information and opinion, so we can assess what's good from what's not. Rather than telling us WHAT to think, Hannah teaches us HOW to think—and with that skill, we are able to fully embrace the goodness of this life.

ERIN STRAZA
Author of *Comfort Detox*
Managing Editor of *Christ and Pop Culture*

ALL THAT'S GOOD

Recovering the Lost Art of Discernment

HANNAH ANDERSON

MOODY PUBLISHERS

CHICAGO

© 2018 by
HANNAH ANDERSON

Unless otherwise indicated, Scripture quotations are from the Christian Standard Bible, copyright © 2017 by Holman Bible Publishers. Used by permission. Christian Standard Bible® and CSB® are federally registered trademarks of Holman Bible Publishers, all rights reserved.

Scripture quotations marked ESV are from The Holy Bible, English Standard Version® (ESV®), copyright © 2001 by Crossway, a publishing ministry of Good News Publishers. Used by permission. All rights reserved.

Scripture quotations marked NASB are taken from the New American Standard Bible®, Copyright © 1960, 1962, 1963, 1968, 1971, 1972, 1973, 1975, 1977, 1995 by The Lockman Foundation. Used by permission. (www.Lockman.org)

Scripture quotations marked KJV are taken from the King James Version, public domain.

All emphasis in Scripture has been added.

Names and details of some stories have been changed to protect the privacy of individuals.

Published in association with the literary agency of Wolgemuth & Associates.

Edited by Amanda Cleary Eastep
Interior Design: Erik M. Peterson
Author photo: Mary Wall
Cover Design: Erik M. Peterson and Faceout Studio
Cover illustration of weathervane copyright © 2018 by AVA Bitter/Shutterstock (635189591).
Cover illustration of horse copyright © 2018 by Yakov Oskanov/Shutterstock (1070034818).
All rights reserved for both illustrations.

All websites and phone numbers listed herein are accurate at the time of publication but may change in the future or cease to exist. The listing of website references and resources does not imply publisher endorsement of the site's entire contents. Groups and organizations are listed for informational purposes, and listing does not imply publisher endorsement of their activities.

Library of Congress Cataloging-in-Publication Data

Names: Anderson, Hannah, 1979- author.
Title: All that's good : recovering the lost art of discernment / Hannah
    Anderson.
Description: Chicago : Moody Publishers, 2018. | Includes bibliographical
    references.
Identifiers: LCCN 2018031608 (print) | LCCN 2018035651 (ebook) | ISBN
    9780802497369 (ebook) | ISBN 9780802418555
Subjects: LCSH: Discernment (Christian theology) | God
    (Christianity)--Goodness. | Aesthetics--Religious aspects--Christianity.
Classification: LCC BV4509.5 (ebook) | LCC BV4509.5 .A5195 2018 (print) | DDC
    248.4--dc23
LC record available at https://lccn.loc.gov/2018031608

We hope you enjoy this book from Moody Publishers. Our goal is to provide high-quality, thought-provoking books and products that connect truth to your real needs and challenges. For more information on other books and products written and produced from a biblical perspective, go to www.moodypublishers.com or write to:

Moody Publishers
820 N. LaSalle Boulevard
Chicago, IL 60610

1 3 5 7 9 10 8 6 4 2

For Phoebe, Harry, and Peter—
May you know how much you're loved.
May you grow strong and brave and wise.
May your lives be filled with all that's good.

Contents

Introduction

"God saw all that he had made, and it was very good."
—*Genesis 1:31*

God, it would seem, had not yet read the morning headlines. Otherwise He would have known, as you and I do, that the world is anything but good. From civil unrest to personal tragedies to spats on social media, the world is full of strife, pain, and confusion. Even on our best days, navigating it can be overwhelming—the sheer number of choices we face dwarfed only by the number of contradictory opinions and data points we must process to make those choices.

Which foods should I eat? Who should I vote for? What school should my children attend? Do I take this job or that one? Does it really matter how I spend my money? Should I stay in this relationship or go? How will I know for sure? Facing so many variables, with good and bad so quickly blurring, most of us find it easier to retreat to safe spaces, cluster in like-minded tribes, and let someone else do our thinking for us. Forget the good life; we just want to survive the one we have.

Of course, the difficulties and dilemmas we face on a daily basis didn't always exist. When God first made the world, it *was* very good—good in its purposes, design, and abundance. Good in its beauty and potential. As good as God Himself is good. And human beings were good too, completely in tune with His good heart.

In fact, when God first made the world, there was no knowledge of anything but goodness. From the redbud trees to the song of the nightingale to the five toes on the left foot, everything everywhere was nothing but good. But like every story, ours had a moment of crisis when the goodness became obscured, darkened by a seemingly impenetrable pall. And so today, you and I must feel our way through the shadows, guarded, uncertain, and afraid.

But what if there were a way to see clearly once again? What if we could see the world as God sees it—in all its brokenness *and* beauty—and in seeing, be able to do more than endure this life? What if we could flourish in it? I think we can. In fact, I'm convinced of this good news: Despite all the pain, all the sorrow, all the questions, goodness still exists because God still exists. And because He does, He has not left us to sort through the mess alone.

I didn't always think this way. For a long time, I didn't think very clearly at all because my actions and choices were shaped more by the brokenness around me than the reality of God's goodness and nearness. When faced with a decision, I played defense: *What will keep me safe? What are other people expecting me to do? What will happen if I make a mistake?*

But in trying to keep myself safe, in obsessing over making the "right" choices, I found myself making a whole lot of wrong ones.

> WHAT IF WE could see the world as God sees it—in all its brokenness *and* beauty—and in seeing, be able to do more than endure this life?

Because I lacked a vision for goodness, I also lacked discernment. And without discernment, I had little chance of finding the security and happiness that I wanted—that I think we all want.

You may not initially connect the idea of discernment with goodness. For some of us, discernment carries a defensive connotation; we see it as a protection mechanism, a shield against the threats of a dangerous world. But in broader usage, discernment simply means developing a taste for what's good. It's developing an instinct for quality, a refined sensibility, an eye for value—to know the difference between what's good and what's not in order to partake of the good. Discernment gives you the ability to both appreciate the subtle beauty of a Renoir and spot a fake. In this sense, cultivating the art of discernment is as much about cultivating the individual as anything else.

Because, whether we like it or not, whether we realize it or not, this is how God works. While He's busy in the world around us, He's also busy in the world within us. As certainly as He has a plan to restore the beauty and goodness of His creation, He has a plan to restore our ability to see and to know it. As the apostle Paul writes in Romans 12:2, He is busy transforming you, renewing your mind "so that you may *discern* what is [His] good, pleasing, and perfect will."

Out of that comes the central question of this book: How can we, imperfect as we are, develop an instinct for recognizing and embracing the good? How does discernment equip us to navigate a broken, complicated world with confidence and joy?

If you're familiar with my writing, you'll know that I don't take

> HOW CAN WE, imperfect as we are, develop an instinct for recognizing and embracing the good?

shortcuts. I won't offer you three easy steps to making good decisions or rigid boundaries to keep you on the straight and narrow. In fact, I'll do my best to complicate your decision-making process, to lead you away from our common disposition to fear-based thinking toward a place of hope and abundance. And while we'll be led by the Scripture, this book is not a systematic theology of discernment or a pastoral guide to discerning God's will for your life. Instead, I think of *All That's Good* as a vision of what our lives might look like were we to be changed by wisdom—if we were to become people who know the difference between what's bad and what's good, what's good and what's better. As with the wisdom literature of the Old Testament, you'll find the content fluctuating between the rational and emotional, the pragmatic and quixotic, the specific and universal—all in an attempt to honor the multidimensional lives we live and the world in which we live them.

We'll start by clarifying what discernment is and, perhaps more importantly, what it is not. Then after laying a foundation for God's good work in the world, we'll explore how fear, pride, and a scarcity mindset can hinder our ability to experience His goodness. This, in turn, will lead to understanding why discernment cannot be separated from virtue—why making good choices goes hand in hand with becoming good people.

But it won't all be esoteric. We'll also examine how contemporary culture undermines discernment—how the dynamics of social media create the perfect environment for con men and groupthink and how insecurity and the need to project a certain image of ourselves ensure that we'll fall for it. But lest any of us escape, we'll also explore why simply reacting to established culture is not enough, why naïveté and isolationism can cause us to misstep just as quickly. Instead, we'll consider how to establish truly countercultural habits that guide us and those we love toward goodness in small, everyday ways. And finally, we'll see how God Himself walks with us, ensuring that all things—even our mistakes—eventually work together for good.

Through it all, we'll operate with an eye toward personal transformation, toward becoming people who know, not just what to think, but *how* to think.

As with my other books, I hope that *All That's Good* will surprise you and take you places you don't anticipate, all in an attempt to make sense of the bigger picture. If *Made for More* and *Humble Roots* offered a guide to the world within ourselves, to what it means to reflect God's glory within human limits, this book will guide you through the world around us, enabling you to navigate life outside the garden. While not necessary to each other, I like to think of these books as singing in harmony, each carrying a different part of the same song—a song of life and abundance, of flourishing and peace, of God's good work in the world and our small part in it.

One last word about the illustrations and aesthetic framing. To help drive home the point that goodness exists and is worth seeking, I'm using experiences, people, and found objects that have been a gateway for me to personally understand the goodness of God. Pearl earrings. A family vacation. Detective stories. The warmth of a fireplace. I suppose in some sense, this book is a list of my favorite things. They often come with a backstory, sometimes even a shadow, and span the ordinary to the ethereal. The variety is intentional because, for those who have eyes to see it, the earth is full of the Lord's goodness.

So come. With David in Psalm 34:8, I invite you to taste and see that the Lord—and all that He has made—is good. Come develop an instinct for all that's true and lovely and perfect and pure. Come recover the lost art of discernment.

I

"And the peace of God, which surpasses all understanding, will guard your hearts and minds in Christ Jesus."

—PHILIPPIANS 4:7

Chapter 1

Taste and See

"A person acquires taste not by accident, but by spending years training his or her eye and learning how to make good judgments." —Letitia Baldrige

It all seemed so straightforward on the internet.

I'd watched one of those time-lapse videos, the ones that record a process from start to finish, like a chick emerging from an egg or a flower opening. This particular video was three minutes long and showed how to decorate pies by cutting and shaping the top crust. Under a perfectly positioned camera, a pair of perfectly manicured hands manipulated a perfectly round ball of dough on a perfectly flourless, shabby chic butcher block countertop. A pinch here, a twist there, a few cuts, and you have a thing of beauty.

The first time I'd seen hands roll out a pie crust was over three decades earlier when I watched my grandmother's experienced hands use a glass rolling pin to roll them out on her laminate kitchen table. The fifth of ten children, she'd been raised in the Appalachian Mountains, where pie was both necessity and art, the understood measure of a woman. When her siblings gathered for a reunion each summer, no one could predict which second cousins and great aunts would be there, but we never wondered whether there would be pie. As sure as the nieces and nephews would play softball and the old men toss horseshoes, we'd eat pie—butterscotch, blackberry, cherry, rhubarb, and chocolate custard.

About two hundred miles due south of where I live now, cake is more the order of the day. Raised in the mountains of this area, my husband, Nathan, shares the regional preference for cake, although he has not yet turned down a piece of pie when I offer it—nor has anyone else. Still, knowing that his heart (and tongue) have been trained to prefer cake, making pie has become something of a personal venture, a skill I curate for the sake of memory and good taste. When I saw a video promising "8 WOW-Worthy Pie Hacks," I bookmarked it for a rainy day.

I like to make pie when the sky is gray and there's a chance of precipitation. A cold drizzle will do, but I prefer a coming storm, the ominous gathering of dark clouds, a perfect foil to the warmth and security of a well-stocked kitchen. A Saturday afternoon is especially good as it's that window of time when the work of the week is over, but the responsibilities of the coming week have not yet descended on our family. Somewhere around two o'clock, after lunch is over and before hunger calls them back, I shoo my children downstairs to where a fire roars in the wood stove and my husband lies dozing in front of a football game. Back in the kitchen, I turn on the radio, make a cup of tea, and give myself to making pie.

One such Saturday came just before Thanksgiving; I pulled up the video on the computer in my kitchen and set to work. Within a few minutes, the dough had come together, and after chilling it, I rolled out several bottom crusts, carefully transferring them to glass pie plates. Then I began the top crusts. For one pie, I cut even strips and wove them under, over, under, over to form a lattice. For another, I braided dough together to ring the outer edge. I cut out decorative shapes and formed small masterpieces, the whole time relishing the sensory nostalgia of bits of dough wedged beneath my fingernails. Soon the pies were ready for the oven.

And that's when the trouble started.

In the video, the step of baking had been reduced to a single screenshot consisting of bold white letters B A K E superimposed over the image of a pie. Easy enough. Form your pie and then simply put it in the oven. But when I checked on them less than thirty minutes later, I discovered that my perfectly sculpted, perfectly pricked, perfectly Pinterest pies had already browned in all the wrong places. To add insult to injury, the bottom crusts remained the pale sickly white of raw dough. The filling that was supposed to simply peek through the whimsical cutouts had boiled up into a blistering flow of fruit lava. What I saw in my oven looked nothing like what I had seen on the video, and it was not good.

À La Mode

This wasn't the first time I'd been frustrated by something online. In fact, whenever I logged on, it increasingly felt like I was navigating a netherworld, uncertain of where the next click would take me or whether it would deliver on its promise. Links to heartwarming stories turn out to be ploys to garner page views. News articles are often nothing more than partisan commentary disguised as journalism. And when I search for treatment for common health problems, the results leave me with more questions than answers. *What if calamine lotion isn't enough to heal a bug bite? What if it's not even a bug bite? What if I wait too long to seek care—what if I've already waited too long? Maybe the answer really is to align my electromagnetic fields and balance my gut bacteria . . .*

When I was a young stay-at-home mom, the internet was a lifeline. From the comfort (and isolation) of my kitchen table, I'd read the news headlines, keep in touch with friends, browse the latest fashion trends, and discover better ways of tackling my daily chores. When Nathan's work took us overseas to New Zealand, email helped us to close the gap between our parents and their year-old granddaughter. Eventually, the connectivity of the digital infrastructure opened doors for me to work from home.

But as technology has advanced and become incorporated into almost every moment of my life, a funny thing has happened. Instead of making life simpler, it often makes it more complicated. Instead of choosing to get online, I now have to go out of my way to unplug. I have to disable alarms on apps, unsubscribe from email lists, and take digital fasts. "Social" media has become decidedly antisocial, the joy of connecting with friends dampened by the inevitable political debates, clickbait headlines, and pop-up ads that dominate my feed. In a single day, I can encounter more data, more opinions, and more ideas than my grandmother did in an entire lifetime.

> IN A SINGLE day, I can encounter more data, more opinions, and more ideas than my grandmother did in an entire lifetime.

Most of the time, my frustration with the digital world is as ethereal as the radio waves that bring it to me: a niggling irritation, a mental and emotional fatigue, a classic love-hate relationship. But sometimes, it has real-world consequences, as when I tried to make my WOW-worthy pies. Or the time I rearranged my week's schedule after a friend posted a weather report predicting eight to twelve inches of snow—a report that was a year old.

In the past, the possibility of changing my plans due to an outdated weather bulletin was relatively low. Forecasts came from a select number of sources: local television and radio stations, newspapers, and for those old enough to remember, telephoning Time and Weather. And while none of these sources could guarantee the outcome of their predictions, I didn't have to question the timeliness or integrity of them.

But over the last decade, smartphones and social media have dramatically changed how we access and share information. Today's digital experience relies heavily on average people like you and me to produce and distribute content. Every Facebook post, every Instagram photo, every Tweet, and every YouTube video adds to the information that's available to other users. Multiply that by an estimated three billion users worldwide, and what was once a welcome source of connectivity and information has become a muddy, torrential flood, sweeping us along with it. As a result, neuroscientist Daniel Levitin observes, "Our brains are busier than ever before. We're assaulted with facts, pseudo facts, jibber-jabber, and rumor, all posing as information. Trying to figure out what you need to know and what you can ignore is exhausting."[1]

In other words, the conflict, confusion, and exhaustion you feel when you log on is the challenge of having to constantly make choices about who to listen to and who to mute, of figuring out which news outlets are reliable and which are driven by partisan agendas. It's the challenge of knowing which of our hundreds of "friends" are true and trustworthy. It's the challenge of needing to realize *before* you invest precious time and energy that a three-minute video probably won't be enough to prepare you to make WOW-worthy pies.

Becoming Wise

Although we experience this informational overload in the context of the digital age, the need to sort through data is not unique to it. New technologies have certainly complicated and altered how we receive and engage with information, but at root, we're facing the same questions that human beings have faced since the garden of Eden: *How can I know who and what to believe? How can I make choices that lead to a successful life? How can I avoid mistakes? How can I know what is good?*

And since the garden, philosophers from Socrates to Hypatia to Gandhi have been trying to answer these questions, to make sense of a world that is often chaotic, manipulative, and quite simply, overwhelming. One of the most famous of these "lovers of wisdom" was Solomon, a king who ruled over the nation of Israel during the tenth century BC. According to scriptural narrative, Solomon encountered his own crisis of knowledge shortly after inheriting the kingdom from his father David. Facing a tumult of political and social unrest, including defending his throne against internal family rivalries (and you thought your Facebook experience was rough), he also had to navigate relationships with neighboring countries and gain the trust of a nation composed of fiercely independent tribes.

Soon after Solomon became king, Jehovah appeared to him in a dream, telling him to ask for whatever he wanted. Foremost on Solomon's mind was his inability to make good decisions. "LORD my God," he replies, ". . . give your servant a receptive heart

> SOLOMON asked for the ability to know the difference between good and evil. He asked for discernment.

to judge your people and to discern between good and evil. For who is able to judge this great people of yours?"[2] Surprisingly Solomon does not ask for sustainable peace or for the challenges of leadership to go away. He did not ask for a long, prosperous reign. He asked for the ability to weigh the challenges he would face and make wise decisions. He asked for the ability to know between good and evil. He asked for discernment.

Broadly speaking, discernment is the ability to sort between a host of options and pick what is good. It carries the idea of judging the merits of something, being able to distinguish between good and bad and what is best. As Solomon writes later in the book of Proverbs, the goal is:

> To know wisdom and instruction,
>   to understand words of insight,
> to receive instruction in wise dealing,
>   in righteousness, justice, and equity;
> to give prudence to the simple,
>   knowledge and discretion to the youth.[3]

In other words, discernment does not change the challenges we face; it changes our ability to face them.

When I think of how quickly the world is shifting around me, I know that I am unable to keep up with it. And while I don't have the responsibility of governing a nation, I understand the weight Solomon felt. With him, I question, *Who is able to do this? Who among us can sort through all the noise? Who can*

> DISCERNMENT does not change the challenges we face; it changes our ability to face them.

survive the waves of new information, new data, and new decisions crashing over us every moment of every day?

But like Solomon, I also know that I can't escape the context I've been placed in. Even if I were to unplug, move off grid, and somehow attempt to isolate myself from the modern world, the modern world would still find me. And when it did, I would be ill-equipped to deal with it. No, as much as we'd like to, there's no going back to a simpler time, no escaping the world we live in. So we must become people who can face it. We must become people who have insight, who can recognize justice and equity, and who can make good decisions. We must become people who can spot goodness when we see it.

Need to Know

But to do this, we first have to acknowledge how much we don't know. And this is where our modern context does present a unique hurdle to developing discernment. Of all of its benefits, one of the drawbacks of the digital age is how easily we mistake information for knowledge. Because we can find the answer to most of our questions, we can begin to believe that we are smarter than we actually are. Because we can find an instructional video to help us perform just about any task—everything from car maintenance to, yes, even making pie—we can begin to believe we can actually perform these tasks.

But tips and tricks are not skill and expertise. Information and data are not wisdom and knowledge. And knowing about something is not the same as knowing how to do it or whether you even should.

If I'm honest, I can't blame a three-minute time-lapse video for how my pies turned out. Sure, the video oversimplified the process of pastry making, presenting an edited version of reality, but I can't escape the fact that *I should have known better.* I'd baked enough pies to know that you have to watch them carefully. I know that you have to rotate them while they're baking and shield the crust to prevent it from burning. I know that any slight change to a recipe—even a change to the shape and design of a crust—can alter the process entirely. No, I couldn't blame the video. The problem was that I wanted the process to be as easy as it appeared online. I wanted to believe that life could be so simple, that all I had to do was follow a few easy steps and everything would be beautiful. I wanted to hack my way to a perfect pie.

In this sense, my desire for a simple solution to a complicated process revealed more about my own simplicity than anything else.

Because here is the difficult truth: there are no shortcuts to skill and expertise. The ability to produce beautiful pies requires more than information—it requires practice and learned proficiency. A video may be able to show me how to do something, but it can't make me a person who can actually do it. Similarly, there are no hacks to discernment. No three easy steps to follow, no lists or tricks or tips to ensure that you'll be able to make good decisions when you need to. In order to make good decisions, you must become a discerning person, a person skilled in wisdom and goodness itself.

And to be these kinds of people, we must be humble enough to be willing to learn.

This is why Solomon continues in Proverbs 2 by calling us to listen "closely to wisdom . . . [to] call out to insight . . . [to] seek it like silver and search for it like hidden treasure" (vv. 2–4). Why he tells us that "the fear of the LORD is the beginning of knowledge; [but] fools despise wisdom and discipline" (1:7). People who do not think they have anything to learn, won't. People who are confident in their own ability to make good decisions shouldn't be.

And people who refuse to humble themselves before the One who is wisdom Himself will never become wise.

But to those who will, to those like Solomon who cry out for understanding, God makes this promise: If you acknowledge your need, if you recognize your inability, if you commit to the process, you will be changed. You will become a person who can face the challenges of this world with clarity, purpose, and confidence.

THIS IS WHAT God does when people ask Him for discernment: He gives it.

Because this is what God does when people ask Him for discernment: He gives it.

Solomon describes God's promise of discernment, saying, "For the LORD gives wisdom; from his mouth come knowledge and understanding. He stores up success for the upright; He is a shield for those who live with integrity" (Prov. 2:6–7). The New Testament writer James confirms this. "If any of you lacks wisdom," he writes, "he should ask God—who gives to all generously and ungrudgingly—and it will be given to him" (James 1:5).

He will not chide you; He will not shame you for all you do not know. He will not laugh at your mistakes or mock your failed attempts. This God, in whom are hidden all the treasures of wisdom and knowledge, this God will simply teach you what you need to know. Out of His generous heart, this God will show you the way of goodness.

Taste and See

We ended up eating my ugly pies because the truth is that no matter what it looks like, pie is still *pie.* My daughter even declared the blackberry one the best I'd ever made, and her compliment was more than platitude. It *was* one of the best blackberry pies I'd ever made, and the reason had nothing to do with what the crust looked like. It was the filling.

To make blackberry pie, I use wild blackberries foraged months earlier. In July, when the sun is high and the days are long, I wander over to a friend's pasture where blackberries grow along the fence row and down to the creek bottom. Once I've picked a few gallons, I come home to make jam, a cobbler or two, and freeze the rest for a time deep in winter when we've nearly forgotten that sun-ripened blackberries exist.

The trick to a good blackberry pie is the texture. You want something firm but not dense, gooey but not runny. Because of their naturally high water content (which is further intensified by the freezing process), blackberries have the potential to produce a soupy mess. And when this happens, the anticipation of slicing through rich flaky crust quickly gives way to the disappointment of having to slurp your pie with a spoon.

But because wild blackberries can be tart, you also have to give attention to your sweetener. A cupful of sugar may be enough or it could be too much depending on the amount of berries, how ripe they are, and the seasonal rainfall. Like texture, getting just the right blend of bittersweetness can be challenging—you don't want a sour blackberry pie, but you also don't want a syrupy sweet concoction that obliterates the tang of the berries.

With both these things in my mind, I had gone to the freezer to discover a further complication: I had only one bag of blackberries left, barely enough for a pie and a thin one at that. So on my way upstairs, I grabbed a jar of blackberry jelly to stretch the berries. Back in the kitchen, I rolled out my crusts, mixed the berries and jelly, adjusted the sugar and thickener, and popped it in the oven. You already know how the crust turned out, but by some culinary miracle the filling was a perfectly firm, perfectly sweet, perfectly

THE GOAL OF discernment is not to simply avoid the evil in this life; it is to learn what is good so that we might embrace and enjoy it.

blackberry foretaste of heaven.

As we look at the chaos of the world around us, it would be easy to count it up as a loss, to see its burnt edges and soggy bottom and simply toss it in the trash, but to do so would be to miss the goodness of the world God has made; to do so would be to miss the best blackberry pie you've ever eaten. Because here is the crux of the matter: the goal of discernment is not to simply avoid the evil in this life; it is to learn what is good so that we might embrace and enjoy it.

Listen to the words of Solomon again:

Then you will understand righteousness, justice,
and integrity—every good path.
For wisdom wwill enter your heart,
and knowledge will delight you.
Discretion will watch over you,
and understanding will guard you.

. . . .

So follow the way of the good,
and keep to the paths of the righteous.[4]

The promise of discernment is the promise of life, the promise that we might reach stability in a changing world. It is the promise that we might have insight in the midst of confusion, that we might find healing in the brokenness. It is the promise that we might taste and see that the LORD truly is good.

Chapter 2

The Good Earth

"Travel, in the younger sort, is a part of education; in the elder, a part of experience." —*Francis Bacon*

Despite being on vacation, we'd been awake since 5:30 a.m., having gotten up before dawn to catch a train. Our family lives in southwest Virginia, about an hour north of where my husband grew up and five hours south of where I did. Even though we were both raised in rural communities and are now raising our children in one, my husband and I love to travel. I suppose we love to travel precisely *because* we grew up in the country, the rural and urban experiences a perfect pairing of sweet and salty, each intensifying the richness of the other. Whatever the reason, my husband and I have been on the go since our early twenties, always looking for a way to visit new places and see new things: New York, Washington, D.C., London, Amsterdam, Munich, Rome, Tel Aviv, San Francisco, and Tokyo.

When children joined our family, we necessarily opted for locations closer to home, but wherever we end up, family trips are a chance to experience all the things we can't at home: art collections, historical sites, and science museums. (I'm afraid our motives are not entirely altruistic. We're not so much good parents as self-interested ones. My husband and I plan trips to places we enjoy, and since we're the ones with the checkbook and car keys, our children don't have much of a choice but to come with us.)

Several hours after our train departed, and just before lunch, it deposited us at the city's main station. We rented a locker, stored our overnight bags, and exited into a maze of unfamiliar streets and traffic patterns. It was a balmy 48°F with threatening gray skies; and of course, we hadn't packed an umbrella. Undeterred, we began to make our way to the city center, hoping to find food as we went.

An hour later, we were still walking. We weren't exactly lost, but we'd misjudged the distance and had to stop at regular intervals to get our bearings. We still hadn't found food that everyone could agree on, and the gray skies had become a steady drizzle. I urged my children on with the promise of dessert after lunch and money to spend in the museum's gift shop, but treats and souvenirs are no match for weather and hunger. They were cold and miserable and quick to invite everyone else into their misery.

It wasn't entirely their fault, of course. They hadn't asked to come on this trip and would have been just as content at home. To be honest, I was beginning to feel the same way. *Is all this hassle worth it?* I wondered. *Maybe we should have saved our money and spent it on a new dishwasher. Or that game system the kids want. At least that would make them happy. Maybe we should have never come; maybe we should have just stayed home.* But instead, there I was dragging tired, cold, hungry, complaining children through the streets of Paris in the rain.

Comfort Zone

"What do you think about flying to London next fall?" Nathan had asked offhandedly one winter evening. "We can even take the train over to Paris if you want."

A few years prior, such a suggestion would have been ludicrous, the fantastical daydream of a person who read too many novels and watched too much public television. During the first decade of our family's life, we moved, on average, every eighteen months. Nathan's career as a pastor was marked by multiple job changes, including an extended period of un- and underemployment, which we survived on public assistance. But we'd been in Virginia several years, and now things were different. While our ministry salary is modest by many people's definition, it is stable and fair, enabling us to purchase our first home and escape the financial drain of renting. Putting down roots also allowed us to tap into the unseen benefits of community—getting a friend to help with a car repair instead of paying a mechanic or being gifted hand-me-downs for boys who never seem to stop growing. Released from the daily struggle to make ends meet, we found ourselves able to dream for our future and work toward it with the hope that we might actually reach it one day.

By the time Nathan suggested we fly to London, we had been saving for a trip like this for several years, putting money aside as we could.

Because as much as we are committed to giving our children deep roots in our community, we also want them to grow upward and outward. We know we'll have to challenge the anxiety that can so easily develop in small places, so we want to show them that larger cities and foreign places and new things are nothing to fear. We want them to know how to navigate a subway map as easily as they can navigate a forest trail.

But when all this beautiful theory was finally put to the test that rainy day in Paris, I wasn't sure I was committed to it. Tired, cold, hungry, and disoriented, I wasn't sure that exploring the broader world was so important after all. In those moments, all I wanted was to be in my reading nook, wrapped in a blanket,

> IN OUR PURSUIT of discernment, the first question we must answer is whether the sacrifice of pursuing it is even worth it.

with a mug of hot chocolate. All I wanted was to be back in Virginia in the comfort of my own home.

In our pursuit of discernment, the first question we must answer is whether the sacrifice of pursuing it is even worth it. And a lot of that depends on whether goodness exists in the first place. As compelling a picture as the Scripture paints of the rewards of discernment, when I lift my eyes from its pages and look at the world around me, I seriously doubt whether it can fulfill its promises. Not because I doubt its intent or its truthfulness, but because the chaos and confusion seem impenetrable: the constant noise of conflicting opinions and positions, the unjust suffering of innocent people, the apathy of government leaders to punish evil and reward good, the moral and ethical failures of *religious* leaders. Even the relationships I hold most dear are a regular source of misunderstanding, conflict, and pain—as traveling together as a family quickly affirms. Sure, a trip to Paris sounds good in theory, but *have you taken children to a foreign country before*? Why even bother?

Not surprisingly, the chaos of the digital age has evoked similar questions from us as a society. Given the challenge of sorting through the noise and fighting to make things right, we're more likely to opt out of the struggle entirely, to retreat into our safe spaces, hunker down, and stay in our comfort zones. We're more likely to remain in what activist and author Eli Pariser has termed our "filter bubbles."

Unique to the digital age, these bubbles are informational

comfort zones created when algorithms craft our online experience to suit us. By collecting information about our likes and dislikes—where we live, what we buy, what we search for—social media platforms and search engines offer, as Pariser puts it, "a unique universe of information for each of us."[1] By filtering out information that we won't find interesting, filter bubbles tailor news stories, search results, and even which friends show up in our social media feeds, all to increase the likelihood that we engage in information that suits our established preferences and opinions. As more of us get our news and opinions from online sources, filter bubbles also mean that we're less likely to encounter viewpoints that challenge or unsettle us.

From the standpoint of search engines and social media platforms, filter bubbles make sense because they allow digital companies to provide a positive, comfortable experience for users—a positive experience that will likely result in continued and increased use. But for users, they present a more complicated question: We may like engaging with those who share our established perspectives, but how does such an individualized approach to information affect us? How does it affect our ability to learn new things? What happens to a person when they just decide to stay at home where they are comfortable?

Fly Away Home

The same years that gave us words like "post-truth" and "filter bubble" also gave us the Danish word *hygge* (pronounced hoo-ga), a popular lifestyle trend that promises happiness through simple comforts—the warmth of a fireplace, hand-knit sweaters, homemade breads, a well-worn novel, the company of family and close friends. In a long-form essay in *The Guardian*, Charlotte Higgins observes that these homey artifacts carry an almost magical quality and "summon up feelings and emotions: of safety and solace, of comfort and calm, of a being-in-a-time-before." Different from the consumerism that some of us leverage to find comfort, Higgins describes *hygge* as "always anti-modern, and always tinged with nostalgia . . . a retreat, an escape, a turning-inwards."[2] In many ways, *hygge*-esque pursuits are natural coping mechanisms in an age of rapid change, proving Blaise Pascal's observation true: "Little things comfort us because little things distress us."[3]

WHILE TECHNOLOGY is hurtling us toward an unknown future, vintage comforts help us enjoy a simpler pace.

While technology is hurtling us toward an unknown future, these vintage comforts help us slow down and enjoy a simpler pace. So while I make pies to connect with my heritage, others learn how to knit, bake, preserve food, carve wood, and stay close to home. Unlike generations before us who used these skills to survive physically, we are using them to survive emotionally. In dramatic irony, we use our smartphones to Google natural remedies, order beard-grooming supplies from Amazon, and post pictures of our homemade jellies and jams on Instagram.

As good as comfort and nostalgia can be, there's a potential pitfall if we try to use them to retreat from the world around us. At best, they can provide us a momentary respite from the pain of modernity. At worst, they can cut us off from true goodness by isolating us from the wider world and each other. Because this is the dark side of an approach like *hygge*: if my ability to navigate the world is based on my comfort, what happens when something or someone makes me uncomfortable? Meik Wiking, the CEO of the Happiness Institute in Copenhagen and author of

The Little Book of Hygge, concedes that *hygge* can become a form of parochialism that "doesn't readily admit newcomers" and further says that "getting into a social circle requires a lot of effort and a lot of loneliness on the way."[4]

In an attempt to protect ourselves, we end up isolated and alone. In an attempt to find comfort, we become anesthetized to true goodness. And in an attempt to avoid the chaos of the wider world, we never get on the train to Paris.

Manhandled

We found a spot for lunch, made it to central Paris, and eventually, with a bit of luck (and the help of a search engine), found our way to the Louvre, bypassing the main entrance in favor of a less frequented one in Place du Carrousel, an underground mall attached to the museum. A snack and a quick talking-to negotiated a temporary peace with the children, just enough time to hit the highlights. At one point, we wandered into a hall of Greek and Roman statues where studies of the human form stretched as far as the eye could see, my children's discomfort from walking in the rain suddenly dwarfed by the awkwardness they felt at seeing so much nakedness depicted so freely and so accurately.

Leaving them to gape for a few minutes, I wandered ahead and came across a statue of a woman kneeling. Her back was toward me, the smoothness of the marble perfectly accentuating the curve of her spine, the fluid composition and skilled craftsmanship lending her body the appearance of softness. Instinctively, I moved toward her, but as I did, I noticed a small mound of marble protruding from her back. At first, it looked like a growth of some kind, entirely at odds with the statue's composition, but then I realized what it was and felt a flood of emotion. It was a small, chubby hand.

It was the hand that once reached up to touch my face with wonder, curiosity, and unashamed ownership. It was the hand that grabbed at my necklaces and played with my hair when I forgot to tie it back. The hand that slowly but surely gained control over its movements, first learning to grasp and then to pinch. The hand that eventually figured out how to hold a pencil, catch a ball, and play the piano. It was the hand that still reaches for me in unfamiliar places—the hand that had all morning clutched for the reassuring presence of my body. It was the hand of a child.

A plaque in front of the statue identified it as *Crouching Aphrodite*, a Hellenistic work from the first to the second century. The composition itself was a popular one for the time: the goddess of love at her bath. But why was this hand on her back? And where was the rest of the statue? In fact, the hand on Aphrodite's back belonged to her son Eros (known as Cupid in Roman mythology) who had come upon her during her bath.[5] Over the millennia, the portion of the statue depicting the child had broken off at the wrist and had been lost. But attached to the main part of the statue, the small, chubby hand survived.

The damage to *Crouching Aphrodite* was not unusual. Many of the statues on display had lost appendages, including two of the Louvre's most famous acquisitions: the *Venus de Milo* and the *Winged Victory of Samothrace* (missing arms and a head, respectively). But their disfigurement is still startling, a testament to how far these works of art have come from what they once were. If you're not careful, the damage can be so distracting that you can entirely miss the goodness of what *is* in front of you.

In his book *The Quality Instinct*, museum director Maxwell L. Anderson suggests that one of the greatest barriers to developing an eye for goodness is that we can't see past the condition of an ancient piece of art. "The untrained eye," he writes, "can lose its way in the pursuit of quality for any number of reasons.

. . . Most visitors to museums have trouble admiring works that have endured damage. . . . I [take] it for granted that wonderful treasures can be manhandled or suffer from the elements."[6]

Manhandled. What a perfect word to describe what has happened to God's good world.

MANHANDLED. What a perfect word to describe what has happened to God's good world.

And It Was Good

Just as it was hard for me to imagine what *Crouching Aphrodite* looked like in her original perfection, it's also difficult to imagine the world when it was not in ruins. But despite our lack of imagination, the Scripture teaches that the world was formed in goodness and is sustained by goodness to this day. In fact, some of the first words in Genesis 1 affirm the goodness of the world around us: "God said, 'Let there be light,' and there was light. God saw that the light was good" (v. 3). Then later, "God called the dry land 'earth,' and the gathering of the water he called 'seas.' And God saw that it was good" (v. 10). Over and over again, God proclaims His creation good—from the first shaft of light that penetrated the darkness to the showy hibiscus to the frilled neck lizard. He looks on it all and behold, it is very good.

Later in Psalms, David proclaims that "the earth is full of the goodness of the LORD."[7] And in his first epistle to Timothy, Paul reminds him that "everything created by God is good, and nothing is to be rejected if it is received with thanksgiving" (4:4). In other words, to reject the goodness of the world around us is to reject the work of its Creator. When we act as if there is nothing of value to discover, we disdain the One who made it. And whether we realize it or not, turning our noses up at the goodness He offers us is what got us into this mess in the first place. According to the Genesis account, after God creates the first man and woman in His image, He places them in a garden that is full of beautiful plants and trees, all good for food—and commands them to partake of its abundance: "God blessed them, and God said to them, 'Be fruitful, multiply, fill the earth.' . . . 'You are free to eat from any tree of the garden.'"[8] Out of the overflow of His good, gracious heart, the Creator of the universe invites His children into the good world He has made. With one caveat: "you must not eat," He says, "from the tree of the knowledge of good and evil, for on the day you eat from it, you will certainly die" (Gen. 2:17).

> ADAM AND EVE saw all that God offered them and decided that it was not good enough.

So, of course, being the children they were, that's exactly what they did.

Genesis 3 records that instead of embracing God's good gifts, the man and woman doubted God's generosity toward them, doubted that an entire world of goodness was enough. Instead, they turned their eyes to the one thing that had been withheld.

> The woman saw that the tree was good for food and delightful to look at, and that it was desirable for obtaining wisdom. So she took some of its fruit and ate it; she also gave some to her husband, who was with her, and he ate it. (v. 6)

Do not mistake what is happening here: As much as the man

and woman clearly defied God's boundary, they also rejected everything He had already provided for them. They saw all that He offered them and decided that it was not good enough. And in doing so, they turned from His goodness to seek goodness elsewhere.

But all they discovered was evil.

Good and Evil

Prior to this moment, the man and woman had only ever known goodness. From the beauty around them to their companionship with each other and their relationship with God as their Creator, all was only good. In turning from Him, however, in removing themselves from the source of goodness, they encountered evil for the first time. But instead of making them wise, it made them foolish; and now aware of both good and evil, they found they could not distinguish between the two. Up became down, left became right, and white and black merged into a foggy gray.

Millennia later, we still live in this same state of confusion. But for all that we can't see clearly, we do know that some things are not as they should be. And the fact that we can even recognize this confirms the reality of goodness. The fact that I stood in front of a broken statue at the Louvre on a rainy afternoon meant that the statue existed. Eros's small plump hand resting on Aphrodite's back meant something too.

In *Mere Christianity*, C. S. Lewis reflects that he had once argued against the reality of God because the universe seemed cruel and unjust. "But how," he wonders, "had I got this idea of *just, unjust*? A man does not call a line crooked unless he has some idea of a straight line. What was I comparing the universe with when I called it unjust?"[9]

Paul uses a similar logic in Romans 7 to explain the tension we feel between good and evil within ourselves. He begins by describing how his desire to do good is often thwarted by his inability to do it. "I do not do the good that I want to do," he confesses, "but I practice the evil that I do not want to do. . . . For in my inner self I delight in God's law, but I see a different law in the parts of my body" (vv. 19, 22–23).

If goodness didn't exist, there would be no struggle.

But there is a struggle. And *Crouching Aphrodite* is still missing Eros. And *Venus de Milo* does not have arms. What are we to do with that? What are we to do with the brokenness?

Standing in the hall of statues, I could not see them as they once were. I could only see them as they were in front of me. But for all that I could not see, I could still embrace them. I could enjoy their goodness because I was learning to discern the work of the craftsman, a work that was present despite the damage.

In the context of learning discernment, Dutch theologian Henri Nouwen describes this as the ability to "'see through' the appearance of things to their deeper meaning and come to know the interworkings of God's love and our unique place in the world."[10] Discernment does not overlook the brokenness of the world. It does not deny its need of redemption. It does not excuse sinfulness, live in a false reality, or pretend that a damaged statue is just as good as a carefully preserved one. What discernment does is equip us to see the true nature of the world and of ourselves—both the good and the bad. Discernment helps us see the world for what

> DISCERNMENT helps us see the world for what it was made to be and believe that God is powerful enough to restore it.

it was made to be and believe that God is powerful enough to restore it to its intended purpose. That somehow we are part of that process. That somehow we will be restored ourselves.

Wrestling with the tension between the good that he wants to do and the evil he actually does, Paul finally cries out: "What a wretched man I am! Who will rescue me from this body of death? Thanks be to God through Jesus Christ our Lord!" (Rom. 7:24–25).

With Paul, I'd be foolish to not recognize and grieve the brokenness. I want to see how the sculptor had composed Eros; I want to see the positioning of the *Venus de Milo*'s arms, to gaze on the noble face of *Winged Victory*. But I also know that it would be foolish for us to construct artificial limbs as a replacement for the goodness of the original. At some point, the only One who can fully and faithfully restore His work of art is the original craftsman Himself.

This is the good news of the gospel, the heart of the Christian faith, the confession of all who believe: a good God sent His good Son to make us good once again.

But as He does, and as we wait, I think it is more than enough for us to look on a broken statue and delight that goodness remains: to see the obvious tenderness of a mother at her bath, to know that her small child reached up to interrupt her. So too, with eyes of faith, we can look at the world around us and discern enough of its original beauty to know that it is good and worth our engagement. With the eyes of faith we can see the work that God is doing in it—the work He is doing in those of us who come to Him seeking to be made good.

Because slowly but surely, He is restoring us. Slowly but surely, He is renewing our minds so that we can once again know all that is "good, pleasing, and perfect."[11]

Venturing Out

We left the Louvre late in the day just as the skies broke into a downpour, a full-fledged *la pluie torrentielle*. Soaked and shivering, we flagged a taxi to take us to the attic apartment we'd rented in the Montmartre district. On the way, all three of the children dozed, lulled to sleep by the stress of the day, the warmth of the cab, and the slow pace of rush-hour traffic. My husband put his arm around me, and I leaned into him, resting my head on his shoulder.

We arrived at the apartment about forty minutes later, ascended dozens of steps, and let ourselves in with the key our hostess had left under the mat. Inside we discovered that another much shorter set of stairs led to a timbered sleeping loft, complete with a skylight. Standing on the small wooden platform that doubled as a bed, I unhooked the latch and popped through the opening. Before me lay the rooftops of Paris. The rain had ended, leaving behind a clear sky and setting sun. One by one the lights of the city began to emerge. To my left, I could see Notre Dame and to my right, the Eiffel Tower. The echo of the television drifted up from the apartment below me where the children were wrapped in blankets, cuddled together watching French cartoons.

I turned to go to them, but as I did, I caught sight of something. Directly behind me, high on Butte Montmartre, was the majestic edifice of Sacre-Couer Basilica, her travertine towers and magnificent domes illuminated against the quickly darkening sky. I caught my breath. I was in Paris. My husband and children were with me. We had warm beds and food. We had made it. And in that moment, I knew that all the struggle, all the effort, all the money, time, and emotion had been worth it.

In the chaos of the world, it's very easy for us to believe that brokenness is ultimate. And if that's the case, then the best thing we can do is find a safe place, gather our loved ones, and hunker down. The best thing we can do is stay close to home. But Scripture offers a slightly different reading. It tells us that God's world—for all its brokenness—is good and worth discovering. But discovering this goodness only comes by sacrifice and faith. Not only must we believe that God exists, we must believe that He rewards those who seek Him. "I would have despaired," David confesses in Psalm 27:13, "unless I had believed that I would see the goodness of the LORD in the land of the living" (NASB).

We do believe. So instead of settling for comfort when goodness is offered, we trust that it's worth the risk of venturing out; it's worth the risk to discover the goodness of God and the world He has made.

We do believe. And we will see His goodness.

Chapter 3

Worldly Wise

"He loves Thee too little, who loves anything together with Thee, which he loves not for Thy sake." —Augustine

I'm not a natural musician, but for a reason known only to God Himself, I find myself sitting at the piano every Sunday morning, banging out hymns and choruses as the members of Small Brick Church sing along. Our congregation is gifted with a wealth of natural musicians who can easily fall into four-part harmony, pluck a melody on a guitar or banjo, and sing an *a cappella* solo in a way that makes you wonder why the piano was even invented. But we don't have as many musicians trained in the skill needed to accompany traditional worship, namely, the ability to read music. So when our main pianist could no longer play, it fell to me.

My relationship with music is complicated. When I was young, my parents paid for nine years of piano lessons, of which I probably practiced four. It wasn't that I didn't like the piano. I spent hours a week pounding out melodies; I just didn't spend hours a week practicing my lessons. Sitting in front of our old cabinet grand, I found an odd and unexpected freedom. I could push a key, and it would do what I told it to. Such power was intoxicating. Sheet music became nothing more than a starting point for my improvisations; I'd spend hours creating musical novelties, completely unfettered by timing, notation, or the basic rules of harmony.

At my parents' insistence, I eventually mastered enough pieces to justify my lessons—a handful of sonatinas and hymn arrangements, Erik Satie's *Gymnopedie No. 1*, and a rough rendering of Carl Philipp Emanuel Bach's *Solfeggio in C minor*, a piece whose main reason for existence, I believe, is for young pianists to impress their parents and prove that they have actually learned something.[1]

When I think about it, though, it's not completely unexpected that I find myself at a piano in church. I don't think any other space would have the ability to draw me back after all these years. I may not be a naturally gifted musician like Aretha Franklin or Johnny Cash, but I do share this with them: our musical education began in church.[2] My first memories of music include standing as a congregation to sing the Doxology:

Praise God from whom all blessings flow;
Praise Him, all creatures here below;
Praise Him above, ye heavenly hosts:
Praise Father, Son, and Holy Ghost.

After the last strains of the Amen echoed through the sanctuary, we'd bow our heads in prayer, and I'd peek at my parents through my fingers. Throughout high school, I sang in church choirs, but because of our religious tradition, my playlist was limited to sacred and classical music—a musical foundation that in its own way was invaluable, albeit somewhat specific. To this day, I struggle to follow a syncopated rhythm, and my knowledge of music post-1950 is patchy.

One way I've tried to expand my musical lexicon is by

collecting old records. Not surprisingly, my record collecting is about as disciplined as my piano playing is. I don't know the proper technique, and my purchasing theory can be best summed up as "whatever catches my fancy." Our record player isn't anything impressive either. It's not vintage, expensive, or even good quality, but, just like the piano of my childhood, it does what I ask it to. I realize, of course, that the digital age gives me almost unlimited access to music, but there's something to discovering musicians in their original medium. And because record players are not particularly portable, listening to records forces me to sit and give attention to the music instead of using it as a soundtrack for other things.

You do have to be careful with old records, though. The likelihood of scratched, warped vinyl means that they may not play once you get them home; you also have to check to make sure that the record inside matches the cover outside. I once bought a Bing Crosby album from a thrift store only to discover (by happy providence) that it had two records by the jazz pioneer Sidney Bechet inside. So instead of listening to Bing croon about Irish eyes, I sit in my living room listening to Bechet's sultry soprano sax, feeling very sophisticated and worldly wise.

Vanity Fair

Even as I venture beyond the musical boundaries of my childhood, I do understand why they existed. The prohibition wasn't against the music itself so much as the larger world it represented—a world marked by greed, lust, addiction, and every kind of excess you can imagine. A world whose prevailing approach to life is "Eat, drink, and be merry, for tomorrow we die." A world that doesn't know the difference between pleasure and goodness.

As we begin to catch a glimpse of the goodness the world has to offer, we could easily ricochet from complete withdrawal to unchecked consumption and indulgence. Because in comparison to the brokenness, anything that brings momentary relief feels good even if it doesn't provide lasting goodness. And so we could find ourselves indulging in the comforts of this life in order to escape the cares of it.

Even Solomon, in all his wisdom, was tempted by this. "I have seen all the things that are done under the sun," he writes in Ecclesiastes, "and have found everything to be futile, a pursuit of the wind. What is crooked cannot be straightened; what is lacking cannot be counted" (1:14–15). There's helplessness to Solomon's words. It's not just the struggle to know what's good and what's bad but the question of whether pursuing goodness makes any difference. *After all, in a world of oppression, toil, and ugliness, why fight against it? Why go through all that work if bad things still happen?*

As he wrestles, Solomon decides to pursue whatever his heart fancies. He writes, "I said to myself, 'Go ahead, I will test you with pleasure; enjoy what is good.' . . . All that my eyes desired, I did not deny them. I did not refuse myself any pleasure."[3] And so despite having learned wisdom and despite having taught it to others, he begins an experiment in excess. Fine wine, excellent cuisine, and high-end entertainment. He buys land and builds a dream house and plants gardens and vineyards. He hires servants to tend to his every need and collects the latest technology and treasure. He lives the life of the international playboy—charming, well-spoken, and adored by lovers. He is sophisticated, elite, and entirely free. He's also entirely unhappy.

Solomon eventually comes to the conclusion that it all was meaningless, that everything he indulged in was "futile and a pursuit of the wind. There was nothing to be gained under the sun."[4] Or as the old King James Bible puts it: "all is vanity and vexation of spirit."

Vanity of vanities. What's the point? Nothing matters.

How is this possible? How can things that initially seem so enjoyable and look so good end up being so unsatisfying in the end? In the Sermon on the Mount, Jesus helps us understand what lies at the root of Solomon's unhappiness—and our own. "Don't store up for yourselves treasures on earth," He says, ". . . but store up for yourselves treasures in heaven. . . . For where your treasure is, there your heart will be also."[5] In other words, the reason Solomon became dissatisfied with consumption, the reason we will also find it unsatisfying, is because it cannot offer the deeper, richer, sustainable goodness that our souls seek. When we invest our hearts in temporary things, things that John describes as "passing away," we must constantly replace them to maintain our joy.[6] And so we're constantly looking for newer, better, faster, and flashier and will gladly pay for them even if we don't need them.

> HOW CAN THINGS that initially seem so enjoyable and look so good end up being so unsatisfying in the end?

Understanding how our hearts relate to possessions helps explain cultures marked by consumerism and driven by the belief that new is always better. Giles Slade, the author of *Made to Break: Technology and Obsolescence in America*, writes that part of what motivates consumers to keep purchasing is that they are in "a state of anxiety based on the belief that whatever is old is undesirable, dysfunctional, and embarrassing, compared with what is new."[7] So in order to be happy, we keep consuming, keep buying, keep indulging—but the whole time, the things we gain leave us empty even as we crave them all the more. We're not victims of planned obsolescence as much as partners in it.[8]

In order to find lasting happiness, we must invest in things that last, we must store up "treasures in heaven." Because what ultimately makes something good is not whether it brings us momentary pleasure but whether it brings us eternal pleasure, whether it satisfies both our bodies and our souls.

Simple Gifts

Unlike modern gadgets that become outdated on release, the technology that allows me to play my Sidney Bechet album is the same basic technology that Thomas Edison patented in 1878. To look at it, a record is nothing more than a hard, flat disk with thin concentric circles, but the circles are actually grooves with microscopic variations that the record needle "reads." The resulting vibrations are translated into electric signals, amplified, and as if by magic, make my living room sound like a 1940s nightspot.

Another surprising thing about records is that while the record itself is spinning in a circle, the needle is actually moving closer and closer to the center with each spin. The circles that appear concentric are really one continuous spiral that begins at the outer edge and slowly loops toward the center.

We often think of life on this earth in a linear fashion, a road that leads straight off into eternity. Because of this, when we think about investing in heavenly treasure or things that last, we could easily assume it means forgoing anything but necessities here on earth, that we should only invest in things of an obvious religious or spiritual nature. But Solomon presents a different vision of our time on this earth—one that simultaneously complicates and clarifies the search for good things.

Having realized that seeking pleasure itself is not good, Solomon began to understand that his problem wasn't so much what he was pursuing as *how* he was pursuing it. He had been pursuing good things apart from God, the Giver of good things. But "apart from him who can eat or who can have enjoyment?" he asks.[9]

This leads Solomon to an equally profound thought: "For everything there is a season," he writes, "and a time for every matter under heaven. . . ."

> He has put eternity into man's heart. . . . there is nothing better
> for them than to be joyful and to do good as long as they live;
> also that everyone should eat and drink and take pleasure in all
> his toil—this is God's gift to man.[10]

What Solomon realizes is that our life on earth, all the things we experience, all the work we do, all the good things we enjoy, aren't simply a hurdle to the next life. They are designed by God *to lead us* to the next life. They are designed to lead us to Him. Like the grooves on a record, God's good gifts are designed to draw us closer and closer to the center, to draw us closer and closer to eternity and Him.[11]

> GOD'S GOOD gifts are designed to draw us closer and closer to the center, to draw us closer and closer to eternity and Him.

But sometimes the record is scratched. Sometimes debris gets lodged in a groove. And when this happens, a record can play on a loop, repeating the same musical phrase over and over and over again, never moving forward. This is what happens when we seek God's good gifts as ends in themselves. When we give ourselves to pleasure without acknowledging God as the source of it, we get locked in an earthly, worldly mindset. We begin to believe that this present moment is all that matters. And we run in circles trying to satisfy ourselves, never getting any closer to where we need to be. Never getting any closer to true goodness.

Instead of forgoing good things in this life, we need to let them do what they were designed to do: draw us toward God.

In 1 Timothy, Paul writes that "everything created by God is good, and nothing is to be rejected if it is received with thanksgiving, for it is made holy by the word of God and prayer" (4:4 esv). Paul is not suggesting that we can indulge in anything we want as long as we pray over it; he's teaching how a posture of thanksgiving and submission to God's Word puts us in a place to know God through His gifts. From this posture, we acknowledge that all good things come down from Him,[12] that without Him, we would have nothing. We submit ourselves to His plans and purposes for our lives, even if they run counter to what the world tells us will bring happiness. And we confess that *He* is our ultimate good.

So that by this turning, turning, turning, this always, only, ever turning toward Him, we will come out right.

Love Not the World

At its essence, worldliness is a disposition of the heart—the belief that goodness comes from the immediate satisfaction of temporal desire. But because worldliness is a disposition of the heart, we can't simply retreat into religious contexts to escape it. We also can't rely on adopting certain positions or practices to avoid it— especially if we use them to avoid the more difficult task of examining our own heart motives. As long as we've picked the "right" education for our children, go to the "right" church, watch the "right" movies, and vote for the "right" candidate, we won't have to face the deeper truth about how easily our hearts are led astray. We could be consumerist, pragmatic, and completely worldly but never know it because we see our choices as "right" and thus are convinced that we are as well.

We see this illustrated over and over again in Jesus' interactions with the religious leaders of Israel. While their commitment to religious practices did not make them hypocrites, their religious practices also could not ensure that they were wise people. In fact, Luke records that while they devoted great care to ritual washing and even made sure to tithe from their herb gardens, they could not discern true justice or love for God.[13] When

> WHEN TRUE wisdom presents itself, people who trust in religious practice will not be able to see it.

Jesus healed a man on the Sabbath, they couldn't decide whether or not this was pleasing to God[14] because they were blinded by their commitment to religious forms. When true wisdom presents itself, people who trust in religious practice will not be able to see it.

No, calling yourself a Christian, inheriting a certain religious pedigree, or having the right network cannot ensure that you are discerning. But perhaps even more frustrating, because religious labels can't tell us whether something is truly good or not, swapping one label for another can't ensure that you'll know what is good either. You may define your life in opposition to everything I just listed—you may disdain the hypocrisy of religious contexts, feel complete freedom in your choices, or reject your Christian upbringing, and none of it has the power to make you any wiser.

So what can? What can we count on to make us discerning people? What can we count on to lead us to what will truly last?

Shortly before His crucifixion, Jesus prayed for His followers, knowing that after He left them, they would be overwhelmed, confused, frightened, and tempted to run. Rather than asking the

Father to preserve them from the challenge, Jesus asks the Father to preserve them *through* it. "I am not praying that you take them out of the world but that you protect them from the evil one," He begs. "Sanctify them by the truth; your word is truth. As you sent me into the world, I also have sent them into the world."[15]

Jesus' logic is counterintuitive to everything we would think. If the world is dangerous, then the best thing to do is withdraw from it. If it's unholy and not to be trusted, then we'd better remove ourselves as far away from it as possible. But instead of withdrawing, Jesus calls His followers to advance. He sends them out. Just as He sent them out into the world at Creation, to take dominion over it and be fruitful, He sends them out into the world to go in His authority and reproduce themselves in new image bearers.

But because the world *is* a dangerous place, they need protection. They need to develop a new set of skills. Instead of changing their circumstances, they need to be changed in them.

Whatever Is Good

When I was called upon to play the piano for our congregation, I wasn't sure how it would go. I knew I didn't have much choice, but I also knew that I hadn't taken lessons for twenty years. I'd played off and on over those years, but not on a regular basis and certainly not in a capacity where other people were counting on me. Despite my concerns, a remarkable thing happened. After several weeks of practice, I found myself to be a better piano player than I was twenty years ago.

I didn't trust it at first. *It must be a fluke. Maybe I don't remember how I played in high school. Maybe we're just singing the easy songs.* But the more I played, the more I realized I actually was a better pianist. Twenty years ago, I could only play a handful of key signatures—two sharps and three flats were my limit, yet when I sit down today, I'm tackling them all (with varying degrees of success, of course). Twenty years ago, I couldn't pick out a melody by ear to save my life; today I can. Twenty years ago, my timing was incomprehensible; today, I have a metronome app on my phone, use it regularly, *and* enjoy it.

The only explanation is that I, and not my piano playing, have matured. Over the years, my ability to focus, attention to detail, hand-eye coordination, and listening skills—all of which are necessary for music—have improved by being exercised in other areas. I can't tell you how it happened exactly. Maybe typing on a regular basis improved my finger control. Maybe juggling family, work, and church responsibilities changed my ability to juggle notes, timing, and technique. Maybe listening for infant cries in the middle of the night improved my hearing. Maybe parenting has given me the patience and discipline I need to practice. Maybe listening to hours of records and exploring new genres expanded my musical vocabulary. All I know is that when I came back to the piano, I felt like a different person entirely.

It's the same with developing an instinct for what is good. You do not develop discernment simply by reading labels, restricting yourself to certain contexts, or following lifestyle rules. You also don't develop discernment by reacting to evil. As James K. A. Smith describes it, this kind of holistic formation is "less about erecting an edifice of Christian knowledge than . . . a matter of developing a Christian know-how that intuitively 'understands' the world in the light of the fullness of the gospel."[16]

> YOU DEVELOP discernment by becoming a person who knows how, not simply what, to think.

In other words, you develop discernment by becoming a person who knows how, not simply what, to think.

Paul teaches this same principle in Romans 12. Calling us to reject worldly patterns of thinking, he writes, "Be transformed by the renewal of your mind, that by testing you may discern what is the will of God, what is good and acceptable and perfect" (v. 2 ESV). But here's the fascinating thing: we learn what is good "by testing," by the process of examining and sorting and paying attention. We learn what is good by judging what things will last and what things won't, by comparing everything we take into our lives to God's standard of goodness.

But because it's difficult to know what goodness looks like, especially if you're unaccustomed to looking for it in the first place, Paul offers this guidance in Philippians 4:8–9:

> Finally brothers and sisters, whatever is true, whatever is honorable, whatever is just, whatever is pure, whatever is lovely, whatever is commendable—if there is any moral excellence and if there is anything praiseworthy—dwell on these things. Do what you have learned and received and heard from me, and seen in me, and the God of peace will be with you.

The genius of Paul's advice is that if we seek these virtues in the things we consume, we will also end up transformed. As Harvard professor and essayist Elaine Scarry observes, "If one pursues goodness, one hopes in doing so to make oneself good. If one pursues justice, one surely hopes to be able one day to count oneself among the just. . . . There is, in other words, a continuity between the thing pursued and the pursuer's own attributes."[17]

Or to put it more pointedly, "where your treasure is, there will your heart be also."

When we pursue whatever things are true, honorable, just,

pure, lovely, and commendable, we are actually pursuing the character of God. When we seek these "treasures of heaven," He will make a way for us to find Him. When we pursue goodness, He will make us good. And suddenly we come full circle. Suddenly we find ourselves in the center of the record. Suddenly we find ourselves changing.

Because of the connection between virtue and growing in discernment,[18] the rest of this book is devoted to understanding the virtues listed in Philippians 4:8–9. We'll examine each in depth, sitting patiently to hear its individual tones and nuance. We'll see how each virtue traces its roots back to God's own nature and how Jesus and Scripture reveal it to us. We'll also see how far we are from these virtues ourselves. And finally, we'll see how God preserves us in this world by making us holy—how He sanctifies us through His Word.

All Blessings Flow

There are four of us, all women, and we stand in a semicircle on the platform. For the moment, I've stepped away from the piano to join them. Someone hits the first note; there's a pause while we all hum it softly to ourselves and find each other. And then as one, our voices rise. As we move from note to note, we listen for each other adjusting our pitch until we find the right intervals to fall into harmony. Without instruments, we feel our way through the song, developing almost a sixth sense for when we're off. In some ways, it feels more like dancing than singing. Our voices bend and twist around each other, moving together through a world of sound. It feels natural somehow. So natural, in fact, that I hardly recognize what's happening. For a moment, I sense a strange disconnect, an out-of-body experience of hearing myself sing. But then, just as suddenly, I remember where I am and what I'm doing, and I give my attention to the music once again.

Just as maturing physically led me to be a better musician, maturing spiritually leads us to be more discerning people. This maturing happens as we seek what is truly good, and then by extension learn to recognize what is not. It happens when we tune our heart to goodness and let that goodness lead us back to the One from whom all these bountiful, abundant gifts come. It happens when these words finally ring true for us:

Praise God from whom all blessings flow;
Praise Him, all creatures here below;
Praise Him above, ye heavenly hosts:
Praise Father, Son, and Holy Ghost.
Amen.

II

"... whatever is true, whatever is honorable,
whatever is just, whatever is pure, whatever
is lovely, whatever is commendable ..."

—PHILIPPIANS 4:8

Chapter 4

Whatever Is True

"Understand this, I mean to arrive at the truth. The truth, however ugly in itself, is always curious and beautiful to seekers after it." —Agatha Christie's Hercule Poirot

By this time, the windows are dark as is the rest of the house. It's quiet except for the sound of the cat stalking about and my husband's rhythmic breathing as he sleeps next to me. The lamp beside my bed offers just enough light to read the page in front of me. My eyes are heavy, but I can't sleep. Not yet, at least. There are only two chapters left, and I must finish them. It's not a matter of want; it's a matter of need. *How could I sleep not knowing? How could I, in good conscience, lay my head on my pillow while the murderer is still at large?*

I've been staying up late with mysteries since second grade when I first discovered a set of hardback books with a bright yellow cover. The cover art always depicted a traditional-looking girl in a less than traditional predicament—ascending a dark set of stairs with nothing more than a candle, coming upon a castle hidden in the woods, opening an attic trunk filled with secrets from the past. Quickly Nancy Drew, with her titian red hair, powder-blue convertible, and overnight bag (packed with an extra pair of pumps), came to define all that was good about woman-hood.[1] Gracious and friendly, she was also intelligent, capable of outsmarting jewel thieves, rescuing trapped heiresses, and uncovering insurance scams—all with enough time left to attend a dance with Ned Nickerson at Emerson College. I was smitten.

By junior high, I'd discovered Agatha Christie's Hercule Poirot, Miss Marple, and Tommy and Tuppence. And it was only a matter of time before I stumbled across Father Brown, Lord Peter Wimsey, and Brother Cadfael. Whether the drama plays out in a great house or a train traveling west from Istanbul, there is something irresistible about a quick-witted, slightly eccentric detective who, with the help of a faithful sidekick, sorts through the mystery that's befuddled local law enforcement—and uncovers a host of hidden secrets, private dalliances, and ulterior motives in the process.

Still, as much as I enjoy a good whodunit, I've always been slightly unsettled by the fact that I do. *Is it right that I take such delight in death and deception? What kind of person thinks up these stories? What kind of person enjoys them?* In a now infamous article published in the October 14, 1944, edition of *The New Yorker*, critic Edmund Wilson suggests that the appeal of mysteries has less to do with their literary quality[2] and more to do with the purpose they serve socially. With its roots in the mid-nineteenth century, the modern detective story didn't enjoy popularity until the decades between WWI and WWII (the same time period that first brought us Nancy Drew). This "Golden Age" of detection coincided with widespread social instability, or what Wilson describes as a world "ridden by an all-pervasive feeling of guilt and by a fear of impending disaster" for which "it never seemed conclusively possible to pin down the responsibility. Who had committed the original crime and who was going to commit the next one?"[3]

In other words, people pick up detective stories because our world is in chaos and we don't know how to navigate it. We pick up detective stories because, if for only a few hours, they allow us to escape the confusion of our real lives for a controlled, carefully crafted world where we can be confident that right will prevail.

We pick up detective stories because despite their gruesome subject matter, they offer us something that is more elusive in our real lives: certainty, resolution, and truth.

What Is Truth?

You don't have to be a student of world history or a fan of murder mysteries to understand why truth is so important to discerning goodness—just look at your social media feed. Unlike the compact boundaries of a village, the digital world sprawls, leaving us with a type of informational vertigo. But it's not simply that we have too much information; it's that we have too little shared reality. Like the characters in a mystery, we don't know what is true and what isn't. We can't agree on who is an expert and who isn't. So more often than not, we simply craft our own reality and can't be bothered with whether we share it with anyone else or not. As author Kurt Andersen notes:

> Today, each of us is freer than ever to custom-make reality, to believe whatever and pretend to be whoever we wish. Which makes all the lines between *actual and fictional blur* and disappear more easily. Truth in general becomes flexible, personal, subjective.[4]

The result is a confusing muddied experience of the world. When my "facts" collide with your "facts," it results in anger, conflict, mistrust, and isolation. Family members blocking and

> IT'S NOT SIMPLY that we have too much information; it's that we have too little shared reality.

unfriending family members. Perfect strangers yelling and belittling each other. Communities coming apart at the seams—not simply because we can't agree on what is good and valuable, but because we can't even agree on what is *true* anymore. And slowly but surely, our separately constructed realities cut us off from each other and lead us to solitude. Surrounded by a mass of people, we feel unloved and misunderstood, for the simple fact that we've created millions of worlds with a population of one.

Because shared reality is necessary to a good, flourishing life, Paul begins Philippians 4:8 by calling us to first seek "whatever is true." The importance of shared reality to a good, flourishing life also explains why the serpent attacked truth from the start and why Jesus links falsehood with murder. "You are of your father the devil," He says in John 8:44. "He was a murderer from the beginning and does not stand in the truth, because there is no truth in him. . . . He is a liar and the father of lies." When the serpent lied to the woman about the consequences of disobedience, he, in effect, murdered her, bringing death and isolation upon the human race.

And when we lie to and about each other, we destroy the bonds of community that sustain life, effectively destroying the people in them.

Just the Facts

In 1930, as the genre of the murder mystery was entering its Golden Age, a set of London-based writers formed The Detection

Club. Writers like Agatha Christie, Dorothy L. Sayers, and G. K. Chesterton gathered to swap professional tips, critique each other's work, and most importantly, enjoy elaborate dinner parties. In classic secret society form, members even swore an oath, purportedly written by Sayers herself:

> Do you promise that your detectives shall well and truly detect the crimes presented to them using those wits which it may please you to bestow upon them and not placing reliance on nor making use of Divine Revelation, Feminine Intuition, Mumbo Jumbo, Jiggery-Pokery, Coincidence, or Act of God?[5]

For the members of the Detection Club, it was paramount that their detectives actually *detect*. They must analyze and think and discern. They must sift through the evidence, and readers must be able to follow the process. After all, if detective stories are to help us make sense of the chaos around us, they have to be possible within our realm of knowledge. So with this oath, the members of the Detection Club made a statement, not only about what makes for a good mystery novel, but about what makes for good epistemology.

Epistemology is a ten-dollar word for the study of knowledge and opinions. It answers questions like: How do we know what we know? How do we discern truth from error? How do we decide which explanations are legitimate and which aren't? But one of the most fundamental questions epistemology asks is: How do we access information in the first place? Does it simply come to us out of the air, or do we receive it through more material means?

Unlike earlier authors whose stories were marked by melodrama and sensationalism, the members of the Detection Club believed that we access knowledge through our physical lives—through our five senses of sight, smell, hearing, taste, and touch.

The detective may have a superior brain, but the information his brain processes is available to everyone. That's what makes the eventual solution so satisfying: it was there the whole time, right before our eyes.

So too when we are pursuing truth, when we are discerning which opinions to listen to and which voices to give credence to, we must begin with physical, factual reality. Truth that cannot be accessed by other people is not truth, and facts that are not provable are not facts. For Christians who believe in divine revelation, this may sound like a form of rationalism that minimizes the importance of the supernatural. After all, don't we walk by faith and not by sight? Aren't we pursuing the "unseen"?

> WHEN WE ARE pursuing truth . . . we must begin with physical, factual reality.

While it's true that God guides us to truth through His Spirit, it won't happen apart from the physical reality that He has ordained for us. After all, we don't have a sensory experience of the world by accident—God made us both spiritual and physical, and we dare not reject either. Because of this, truth must be rooted in factual reality. Facts are not the sum total of all that is true, but truth is not a set of privately held beliefs that cannot be tested by other people. The information that we use to come to our decisions must be available to them, and we must be prepared for our decisions and opinions to come under scrutiny. We must not be offended when people ask us to prove them. We must not expect people to accept them simply because *we* arrived at them, nor should we accept anyone else's opinions simply because they claim that they are true.[6]

Basing truth in objective reality—making sure that we check

our facts, do our research, and confirm the truthfulness of something before we accept it—does not minimize the importance of the unseen realm. But it does safeguard us from letting our private, personal experience of the world dominate. This can happen in a hundred different ways, large and small. Maybe you have a go-to website that you count on to offer insider information—information that no one else seems to have. Or maybe you have a favorite Bible verse that regularly inspires and encourages you, but when you actually look it up in context, you find out that it means something different than what you thought.

For example, we often quote Romans 8:28 to each other in times of crisis: "We know that all things work together for the good of those who love God, who are called according to his purpose." What *we* mean is something like, "Every cloud has a silver lining," or "You can't have a rainbow without a little rain." But when you continue reading in verse 29, you discover that God means something else entirely: "For those he foreknew he also predestined to be conformed to the image of his Son." In other words, God's idea of what is good for us is often different from our idea of what would be good for us. God intends to make us holy, and He will use whatever it takes to reach that good—including suffering.

If we don't have a strong commitment to reality outside our own feelings and opinions, we can end up living in a false reality. In this reality, whatever we feel or believe to be true becomes truth for us.

Applied to decision making, it's not uncommon to associate discernment with some vague, sixth-sense, gut-level instinct, or hidden knowledge. We think being "discerning" means somehow feeling our way through the world. When questioned about why we came to a certain conclusion, we say things like:

"God told me."

"I have peace about it."

"I feel like it's the right thing."

"I don't think God would do XYZ."

"I just *know*."

Or as T. S. Eliot, himself an ardent fan of detective stories, puts it: "When we do not know, or when we do not know enough, we tend always to substitute emotions for thoughts."[7]

And this is the real danger: when objective truth does not bind us together in community, something else—something less stable—will.

True Feelings

The desire for community is so strong in the human heart that when shared facts and values don't unite us, we will find consensus through shared emotional or subjective reality. We will retreat into tribes that validate our own experiences and form community around these biases and identities. And when this tribal or party identity is threatened, we will respond, not from carefully considered decisions made for the common good, but from a place of insecurity. In the world of a mystery novel, this tribalism is the mob beating down the door of an innocent man because, more than anything, they want to satisfy their need to resolve the crime.[8] They don't hate the innocent man, but they hate the uncertainty of not knowing—and they will sacrifice him (and truth!) to make themselves feel safe again.

What keeps that man from being hanged is the detective producing evidence that proves his innocence.

In much the same way, factual evidence must check our tendency to be swept up in a wave of emotionalism. It's not that emotions are bad—indeed, they are good gifts from God. But emotions alone cannot guide us to truth. Our fear might be able to tell us that *something* is wrong, but it cannot tell us what is wrong, how or why it happened, or even who is to blame.

In the wake of September 11, 2001, the Manhattan Transit Authority developed a campaign to help identify potential terrorist attacks before they happen. The slogan "If you see something, say something" became so popular it was soon emblazoned on posters in subways, bus stations, and airports around the country; public service announcements aired on TV and radio. The goal was simply to enlist the public to identify threats to our communities. There's only one problem: the public hasn't been trained to know the difference between what a valid threat is and what it isn't. *Is a box sitting at a doorstep a bomb? Or did the mailman just deliver a birthday gift from your parents? What about your new neighbor who just emigrated from Syria? Is he a threat, an enemy inside the gates?* Ultimately, the campaign relies on personal discomfort, rooting the decision about what to report within the experience and feelings of the individual. This results in an exceptionally high number of false reports and has the potential to encourage racial and ethnic profiling. It also keeps the public in a constant state of suspicion and alarm. Yes, we must be aware of potential threats, but without facts, our fear and ignorance can trap us in a state of perpetual anxiety.

> IT'S NOT THAT emotions are bad—indeed, they are good gifts from God. But emotions alone cannot guide us to truth.

The problem is not our emotions; the problem is that we are relying on our feelings to do something that they were never intended or equipped to do. Our feelings cannot tell us when

> WE ARE RELYING on our feelings to do something that they were never intended or equipped to do.

someone is a true threat to our safety. Because of this, pursuing truth will require being painfully honest with ourselves. Before we judge someone else's words or actions, we must judge our own understanding and reaction to them. We must let truth penetrate our "inward parts."[9] This requires more than simply repressing or denying our emotions; we must do the harder work of identifying and acknowledging the role our emotions play in our decisions. We must acknowledge that we are not immune to prejudice and fear. We must question our gut responses and compare them to external reality. Like I tell my children, your head and your heart must talk to each other.

To understand what this looks like in practice, consider what happens when your favorite politician or Christian leader comes under scrutiny. If our understanding of truth is rooted in tribal loyalty, we will immediately rush to defend "our guy" without considering the merits of the debate. Instead of carefully weighing each argument, we will caricature the opposition and build straw men we can easily defeat. The whole time, we're sacrificing truth for a more immediate sense of unity and cohesion.

On the other hand, pursuing truth forces us to critique our emotions, to test our loyalties and aversions. To ask:

Why do I like or not like this particular person?
How does my emotional response to her cloud my ability to think about the situation?
Is my aversion rooted in actual fact?
Have I simply been told to dislike him?

Why do I feel threatened by her opinion?

What is underneath my reaction?

Is it because she introduces new ideas that I don't have an
answer for?

If we don't allow truth to pierce our internal process, we run the
risk of letting our feelings about another person trump the reality
about their actions. We will either demonize them or be duped by
them. Our aversion can keep us from embracing and enjoying the
good things that they have to offer while unquestioning loyalty
can blind us to falsehood and leave us open to manipulation.
As much as the detective must separate her personal dislike of
someone from the facts of the case, she must also be willing to
entertain that even her most trusted friend or lover could be guilty
of the crime.

And doing this requires a commitment to truth that supersedes
the relationships and structures that we normally trust to keep us
safe. This kind of commitment to truth will test and unsettle us
in ways we can't anticipate and prefer to avoid. But as Flannery
O'Connor famously quipped, "Truth does not change according
to our ability to stomach it."[10] No, this kind of commitment to
truth will both reveal and build our character.

The Honest Truth

Besides taking an oath to limit their detectives to objective reality,
the members of the Detection Club also committed themselves
to ten rules of "fair-play." Some rules were so apparent, you'd
think they could almost go unstated—Rule #7 for example: The
detective himself must not commit the crime. But like the oath
in which they disavowed "Jiggery-Pokery," Rule #7 holds a deeper
truth: our character affects our ability to uncover and know truth.

At a purely practical level, a detective story cannot have a main character whose private motivations would prevent him from actually solving the crime. Rule #7 is nothing more than the observation that we cannot "serve two masters"[11] or that a double-minded man is "unstable in all his ways."[12] But these axioms reveal something else about the nature of truth.

While truth is based on facts, it involves more than facts and does not end with them. The detective must root her observations in reality, but *solving* the case means making sense of reality. As she sorts through the facts, she must know which are important and then coordinate them into a plausible theory. She needs a way of looking at the facts that explains them. She needs a truthful frame.

This is why pure rationalism and scientism cannot lead us to truth; such approaches cannot tell us how to interpret, arrange, and discern the meaning of what we see, touch, feel, taste, and hear. Nor can they ensure that we will be ethical in the process. Pursuing truth requires more than knowing where the facts lead. It requires the honesty to actually follow them, regardless of who they implicate.

In this sense, truth is holistic; it relies on both the material and immaterial. And it's why Christians believe that divine intervention is necessary to perceive and understand truth. Christianity does not give us access to a "higher truth" so much as it gives us the moral integrity we need to embrace truth. Rather than relying on our own wits, Christians believe that the "eyes of [our] understanding"[13] are enlightened as we submit ourselves to the One who is truth Himself. Humility—not little gray cells—makes us wise.

In the same passage that Jesus asks the Father to sanctify His followers so they will be able to advance into the world, He promises to send the Spirit of truth to "guide [them] into all the truth."[14] He will do this primarily by making sense of what Jesus has already taught them—what they cannot at that moment understand. And He will make sense of it by purifying them.[15] The Spirit of truth will change them to become people who can receive and understand truth in the first place.

Because finding truth relies on the character and integrity of the one handling the facts, how someone handles information can also be a good indicator of their character. A detective who hides evidence, reinterprets obvious facts, or throws suspicion on innocent people is not a detective who can be trusted, even if he carries the title of detective. So too simply carrying the title of "Christian" is not enough to ensure that we are truthful people. Because finding truth depends on both fact and virtue, it's entirely possible for a person who lacks virtue to leverage facts—even religious or theological facts—in an untruthful or false way. As Mark Noll puts it in *The Scandal of the Evangelical Mind*, it is entirely possible for someone to appear to be "honoring the Scriptures, yet interpreting the Scriptures . . . in ways that fundamentally contradict the deeper, broader, and historically well-established meanings of the Bible itself."[16] It's entirely possible for someone to take truthful things and apply or manipulate them in such a way that makes them *functionally* untrue.[17]

Such falseness knows no bounds—conservatives, progressives, and people of every stripe and every political persuasion can be tempted to misuse facts for our own interests. Conversely, if we are not discerning and do not understand the role that virtue plays in discovering truth, all someone has to do is declare something "loving" or "biblical," and we will be taken in by it.

No, it is not enough to quote Bible verses, cite data, or proclaim a certain position to be true. We must be willing to test, question, doubt—not the truth, but our own certainty and our own motivations. We must expect and even invite the Scripture and other people to confront and question us. We must allow truth to make us honest people.

But this is where the difficulty comes. As much as the villagers want the murder resolved, they don't particularly like the detective's prying. As much as they want things to return to normal, they do not want *other* secrets uncovered. They do not want their illicit affairs, double lives, private addictions, and long-held prejudices to come to light. And when someone is looking for truth, no falsehood is safe.

As much as we want other people's sins exposed, we must be willing to have ours exposed too. We must be willing to admit when we've misjudged, misunderstood, and misapplied. We must not be afraid of good, honest, uncomfortable questions because ultimately good, honest, uncomfortable questions will lead us to a richer, deeper understanding of truth and ourselves.

> TRUTH WILL not leave us alone. It will not allow us to be less than God intends us to be.

And this is how truth leads to goodness. Truth will not leave us alone. It will not allow us to be less than God intends us to be. It will press and pull and stretch us. It will force us out of the shadows, out from behind closed doors into the freedom and light of day.

Making a Full Confession

When I pick up a mystery, I can always count on knowing the truth when I turn the final page. But before it ends, a few things must happen. The detective must uncover what happened, and then he must reveal it to everyone else. Sometimes this plays out at a rapid-fire pace. With only pages left, the hero races to catch the culprit before he flees or murders yet again. Sometimes the resolution is more elegant—the detective gathers the main players in a room and walks them through his process, which climaxes with a dramatic and unassailable finger pointed at the murderer. And more often than not, when this happens, the murderer makes a full and dramatic confession.

I've always wondered about this. What's the significance of "the confession"—why tell readers about it or, worse, devote paragraph after paragraph to a self-important monologue? If you have the evidence, why is a confession even necessary? Here is the benefit of the full confession: confession establishes truth for the community and provides resolution. It does not change the past, but it does allow for a future. It allows for healing and hope. By restoring shared reality, it allows us to experience goodness once again.[18]

So too when we speak truthfully about our own actions—no matter how horrendous—we turn our eyes toward the future. People who blame others, make excuses, minimize, or deny their guilt will be forever bound by the past. People who confess and speak truthfully about their actions set themselves and everyone else free.

And this is why we must confess truth both corporately and individually. Why faith cannot be a matter of private belief. Why we must speak truth to and with and about each other. Confessing the truth about who we are and who Christ is unites us, allowing us to move forward into hope and restoration. As Paul writes in Romans 10:9–10:

If you confess with your mouth, "Jesus is Lord," and believe in your heart that God raised him from the dead, you will be saved. One believes with the heart, resulting in righteousness, and one confesses with the mouth, resulting in salvation.

As humans, we long for truth to be established. We long for the peace that comes from a shared sense of reality. We long to be delivered from our own falsehoods, to live openly and vulnerably with each other. And the only way this can happen is if we do not forsake truth. We must bind it about us and write it on the tablet of our hearts.[19] We must be willing to test everything by it. We must be willing to be changed by it. Because only in the light of truth can we be safe; only in the light of truth can we know what is truly good. And only in the light of truth can *we* be known and made good once again.

Chapter 5

Whatever Is Honorable

"A good name is to be chosen over great wealth; favor is better than silver and gold." —Proverbs 22:1

A large oil painting hangs over the piano in my living room. Titled *Red Bank*, the roughly 40" x 38" composition consists of multiple shades of Tuscan red, burnt umber, and blue and yellow ochre but no clearly discernible shapes. A tag on the back tells me that it was completed in 1968 by the southern landscape artist Carl Blair and that it once hung at the National Endowment for the Arts in Washington, D.C. This isn't too surprising. Blair was an up-and-coming modern artist during this period, and his works have since been exhibited internationally, hung in corporate collections, shown in national and regional museums, and as of two years ago, displayed in my living room.

Born in Kansas during the Great Depression, Blair's roots were much more humble. Having grown up on his family's farm, he spent his days working and playing with his cousins along a creek bank. "If I know anything," he'd say, "it is the land and the animals."[1] But while studying at the University of Kansas in the early 1950s, Blair encountered artists like Paul Cezanne and Vincent Van Gogh, and his already unique style became decidedly more so. Simultaneously sophisticated and earthy, Blair eventually settled down to a quiet, steady life as an educator and advocate for the arts in South Carolina. That's where *Red Bank* and I initially crossed paths.

I was about ten when I first saw it hanging in my grandparents' bedroom, its rich hues and creative forms decidedly at odds with the cautious mauve and cream of the floral wallpaper underneath it. It puzzled me. *The title says* Red Bank, *but where is the bank exactly? Is that section of blue supposed to be a creek? And that stroke of yellow a tree?* My reaction to Blair's work was not unusual. His abstract landscapes hit the market at a time when audiences preferred realism. Critics appreciated him, as proved by the spate of awards and prizes he won, but it took the average viewer time to warm up to his way of seeing the world. When friends and family encountered *Red Bank* in my grandparents' home, they knew enough to respect it, but like me, they struggled to understand it. Our collective discomfort was eventually diffused by someone telling a joke about Blair being colorblind, which he was.[2] Blair himself called his work "visual poetry," and while the painting that hangs above my piano is earthy, subtle, and suggestive, his later work is brightly colored, joyful, and vibrant—much like that of Cezanne and Van Gogh.

I inherited *Red Bank* when my grandmother downsized to an apartment after my grandfather's death. But the real story is how they acquired it. My grandfather brought it home one day in the early 1990s when he was working as an in-house printer in South Carolina. His supervisors had decided to redecorate the office and were swapping outdated fixtures for new ones. New carpet, new drapes, new furniture, new artwork.

Not knowing what it was, someone had sent *Red Bank* out with the trash.

Honor to Whom Honor

That a painting could be displayed at the National Endowment for the Arts only to find its way to the garbage thirty years later tells you all you need to know about the next thing that Philippians 4:8 tells us to seek. After calling us to truth, Paul calls us to find whatever is "honorable" because, left to our own devices, few of us can recognize what deserves our respect and attention and what doesn't. Like the unfortunate interior decorator, we tend to celebrate whatever is currently *en vogue,* carried along by the cultural trend of the moment.

In its most basic sense, the word "honorable" carries the idea that something has weight or gravity. When we honor someone, we respect the value and significance of who they are, what they've done, or the position they hold. They, in turn, are considered honorable when their choices are consistent with the significance of their identity, work, or office. Paul uses the same word to explain how church leaders should conduct themselves—both men and women are to carry themselves with a dignity and gravitas that fits their callings.[3] To seek honorable things, then, is to pursue things that have inherent value, weight, and significance.

> To SEEK honorable things, then, is to pursue things that have inherent value, weight, and significance.

This virtue is especially important in a time of rapid change that pressures us to keep up with each new development in technology, fashion, music, entertainment, politics, and social media. Each day, we wake up to a set of new voices, new companies, new names, and new products, all vying for our time, money, attention, and even our worship. Asking questions like "Does this deserve my attention? Does this deserve my respect? Does this deserve my time?" disrupts these cultural forces long enough for us to entertain the possibility that not every innovation is an improvement, celebrities do not automatically deserve our consideration, and the latest news story may not be worth reading. We may not yet have figured out what *is* honorable, but we've stopped long enough to get our bearings.

Asking these questions can also open up new ways for us to think about how we try to keep *ourselves* relevant and how this can potentially undermine good decision making.

Image Crafting

In the age of selfies and social media, one of the most common ways that we pursue personal honor or relevance is by projecting a persona that appeals to our particular community. In itself, this "image crafting" is not new, but the digital age facilitates it in a way that previous eras didn't. When communities are primarily comprised of people who share physical space with each other, it is hard to control what people see of us. We can try to maintain a certain image—the plastered smile, the well-regulated children, the forced familiarities and compliments—but the possibility of being caught off guard is very real.

In digital communities, however, we choose when and how to interact with each other. With a few clicks, a snap, and a swipe, we can manage what other people see; if we guard our image carefully enough, we can cover our flaws and accentuate our assets. We are not lying about our lives so much as editing them to present only what aligns with the preferences of our audience.

Image crafting takes as many forms as there are audiences to perform for. In spaces that honor academic achievement, we'll make sure that our social media handle includes the appropriate letters after our name. (In places that reward marriage and family, we'll make sure to include the appropriate letters *before* our name.) For contexts that value introspection and spirituality, we'll post pictures of an open Bible and cup of coffee. And in an ironic twist, for contexts that honor transparency, we can even begin to perform at authenticity itself. Because transparency is rare in an age of image crafting, it's also valuable, and exposing our unfiltered self can become a way to seek approval. To signal how little we care about what people think of us, we will parade our faults. We'll storm and swear and delight in disrupting established norms—all while performing to audience expectations.

The main reason we participate in our own objectification is because it rewards us. Each like, each positive comment, each retweet and share confirms that we are valuable and worthy of honor. But the opposite is also true. As much as we enjoy positive feedback, think how quickly and radically your emotions shift when someone responds with a rude or negative comment. For some of us, it makes us want to get off social media entirely; for others it draws us deeper into it, causing us to fixate on having the final word. We feel embarrassed, confused, hurt, and even angry.

Why does it bother us so much? Why does someone that we may not even know have so much power over us? Why can't we, despite our best intentions, just walk away?

Part of what we're experiencing is the weight of public shame. As much as social media has given us the ability to gain approval from hundreds of people, it also provides opportunity for us to be embarrassed in front of hundreds of people. It's not that one person has rejected us; it's that they've rejected us in front of everyone else. And should they be able to sway public opinion against us, we face the real possibility of being ostracized. We face the very real possibility of being sent out with the trash.

That's why it's so important to find our source of honor and value in something other than people's opinion—to seek what is truly honorable. If we don't, our decision making will be skewed by a constant attempt to perform for them. Instead of having the clarity to weigh whether something is truly good, we'll focus instead on whether other people perceive it to be good. Instead of asking, "Is this good?" we'll ask:

What will other people think of me if I do this?
What will they say when they find out I went there?
How does sharing this article or product reflect on me?
Will he be upset if I say I don't agree with him?
Will *she* be upset if I do?

And just like the Pharisees, we very quickly begin to make our choices about what is good to be seen by others.

Image Crafter

When I think about how image crafting affects our decisions, I can't help but think of *Red Bank*. When Blair first entered the art scene in the late 1950s, he was painting for an audience that preferred realistic art and didn't understand his contemporary, abstract vibe.

> WE NEED A source of honor that is not dependent on how people perceive us.

But Blair was also a man of faith, a devout Christian who believed that each artist needed to develop the talent and perspective that he had been given. In his career as an educator, he didn't ask pupils to mimic his style; he expected and equipped them to develop their own. Because of this freedom, Blair was able to go beyond what was socially approved to what was truly good.

In order to become discerning people, we also must separate our need for approval from our decision making. But to do that we'll need a source of honor that is not dependent on how people perceive us. We'll need a source of honor that doesn't rest on presenting just the right look at just the right moment. And we find that honor, not in image crafting, but in the One who first crafted us in His own image.

Psalm 8:5 tells us that when God formed mankind in His likeness, He crowned us "with glory and honor." From His own unlimited glory, He places on us an "eternal weight of glory."[4] Even though we are not yet what we should be, we know what we were meant to be—we know the dignity, authority, and gravity of being made like Him. (And when we know that our worth comes from God, it frees us from needing to seek it from other people.) Instead of worrying about pleasing people with our choices, we're free to approach decisions with clarity and courage, seeking good even if it disrupts status quo. But knowing that God has honored us by placing His image on us also inspires us to conduct ourselves in a way that is worthy of it. Through it, we learn both to honor our own God-given identities and to honor those around us.

> WHEN WE encounter someone who holds a viewpoint we don't agree with, we can begin to view their whole existence through the lens of our disagreement with them.

In our current polarized culture, it can be tempting to disdain people who believe and act differently than we do. In a 1991 essay exploring how secular intellectuals view Christian fundamentalists (and vice versa), anthropologist Susan Friend Harding coined the phrase "Repugnant Cultural Other" to describe how easily we divide ourselves into categories of "us" and "them" and then proceed to stigmatize "them."[5] When we encounter someone who holds a viewpoint we don't agree with, we can begin to view their whole existence through the lens of our disagreement with them. Instead of getting to know them and engaging their ideas, we assume that we already know them because we know where they stand on a certain political or religious question. And the degree to which we disagree with them on this question becomes the degree to which we will disrespect and disregard their humanity. They become our cultural enemy with whom we can't imagine having anything in common. We can't imagine that they, like us, are people who love their families, walk their dogs, work hard at their jobs, enjoy a good book, and might just be working toward the common good (even if we disagree about what "good" looks like). By separating ourselves into categories of "us" and "them," we can justify mocking them, misrepresenting their views, and (in extreme cases) condoning violence against them. But "when we engage in dehumanizing rhetoric or promote dehumanizing images," writes sociologist Brené Brown, "we diminish our own humanity in the process."[6]

[If we are to seek whatever is honorable, it must include seeking the honor that is inherent in God's image bearers.] We must recognize their intrinsic dignity and hold it in high esteem. There is no wiggle room on this. No matter how different a person may be from us, no matter what political, social, or moral views they may hold, no matter how strongly and vehemently we disagree with them, no matter their crimes, we must not dishonor the image of God in them. To joke about their death or destruction, to celebrate their pain and loss, to openly mock and belittle their struggles is to blaspheme the God in whose image they are created.[7]

This is no easy thing—especially when someone is not living honorably themselves, when they are not living in a way that is consistent with their identity as an image bearer. Somehow their hatred, pride, and deceit are able to draw parallel hatred, pride, and deceit from us. That's why in his first epistle, Peter makes a point to call slaves to honor unkind masters, wives to honor unbelieving husbands, and all to honor the emperor—an emperor who at that very moment was seeking their lives.[8] In calling us to honor those who have, in all human logic, forfeited the right to honor, we testify to a greater reality: whether or not a person is living within the dignity of their identity as an image bearer does not change the fact that God has bestowed dignity on them.

In honoring them, we honor God.

Expert Testimony

The public's initial response to Blair's paintings was about as mature as mine at ten years old. It wasn't rooted in whether or not *Red Bank* was a good painting, but in our confusion at looking at it. We didn't understand it, and not understanding it made us feel small and uncertain. To alleviate the discomfort, we dismissed its importance.

In his book *The Death of Expertise,* Tom Nichols notes how often this same insecurity can lead us to dismiss experts in fields that we haven't actually studied or know much about. We hate the notion that other people might have more insight on a topic because it makes us feel "less than." "We want to believe we are capable of making all kinds of decisions," he writes, "and we chafe at the person who corrects us, or tells us we're wrong, or instructs us in things we don't understand."[9] Instead, we opt for a form of epistemological equality that deems all ideas and opinions on all subjects equally valuable. While this posture has existed since the first man and woman resisted God's wisdom, the digital age provides an environment for it to flourish.

Having lowered the boundaries of time, space, and (to a degree) socioeconomics, the internet has also leveled traditional sources of information like the academy, professional associations, and even churches. Anyone who has a will to make their voice heard on a given topic now has a way. But this means that by simply garnering enough page views and likes, the opinion of the latest celebrity guru can hold as much weight as the PhD with thirty years of experience. Talk show hosts have more credibility than lifelong civil servants. And your great aunt's opinion about the correct interpretation of a Scripture passage is as valid as your pastor's. At best we dismiss those who have academic and professional credentials; at worst, we're suspicious of them precisely because they do have them and only rely on them when we absolutely have to.

The human tendency to not honor experts may be part of the reason that Paul writes in 1 Timothy that church elders who rule well should "be considered worthy of double honor" (5:17). Compared to surrounding Greco-Roman society, the early church was remarkably egalitarian. Here rich and poor, slave and free, Gentile and Jew, men and women worshiped God freely and equally. Pushing back against cultural inequities, the risk was not that church leaders would be honored too much but that they wouldn't be honored in proportion to their expertise and unique calling. Precisely *because* the members of the Body were all equally valuable, it would be tempting for members to conflate their individual gifts and roles with the distinct position that elders hold as those devoting their lives to Christ's flock, both spiritually and literally.[10] Paul makes a similar argument in 1 Timothy 6:2 regarding the relationship between believing servants and masters: instead of giving us permission to disrespect each other, our relationships in Christ call us to *greater* respect and care of each other. The fact that we are brothers and sisters doesn't nullify our responsibility to honor each other; it increases it.

At the same time, it's important to note that receiving "double honor" depends on whether the elder has ruled well—on whether the elder is truly an expert in the gospel. Only a few chapters earlier, Paul gives extensive qualifications for church leaders, including that they have proven character and be "above reproach" (1 Tim. 3:2). To be worthy of double honor, an elder must also accept the responsibility of intensified scrutiny, of knowing that with great privilege comes greater accountability.

Ultimately, as much as deriving honor from our identity as image bearers frees us from having to impress people, it also frees us to learn from experts without feeling threatened by them. Because my sense of worth is safe, I can open myself up to new ways of thinking about things, knowing that even experts are accountable to God. If, on the other hand, we indulge our anxiety, we will guarantee that we remain ignorant of the good things that experts can teach us. But perhaps the most ironic consequence of resisting experts is that we end up contributing to a culture that will resist hearing us when we speak from our own expertise.

R-E-S-P-E-C-T

Red Bank isn't the only significant painting that hangs in my home. I also have a painting of a local cow done by a friend who's a public school art teacher and a "Bob Ross" acrylic done by my husband's grandfather during his retirement. And I have a rotating exhibit in my kitchen that regularly debuts fresh, young artists. None of these quite reach the technical quality or impressive provenance of *Red Bank,* but they deserve honor nonetheless. They deserve to be mounted, framed, and appreciated for what they are—for what they contribute to my home that *Red Bank* never could.

As much as populism does not give honor to whom honor is due, elitism doesn't either because it says that only those with wealth, education, social standing, and political influence are worthy of honor. It says that *only* expert opinions matter. But elitism fails to recognize that we're all experts in *something*. As much as a doctor is an expert in medicine, a mother is an expert in the child she brings to him. As much as a newly arrived pastor may be an expert on church practice, a faithful church member is an expert on this particular congregation. If either refuses to honor the expertise of the other, they will both miss goodness.

Unlike elitist paradigms, God regularly upends our cultural notions about who and what deserve honor, choosing instead to "destroy the wisdom of the wise."[11] Instead of using the rich, He uses the poor. Instead of celebrating the powerful, He celebrates the weak. And instead of calling those of noble birth, He sends His Son to a manger. "Brothers and sisters," Paul writes, "consider your calling: Not many were wise from a human perspective, not many powerful, not many of noble birth. Instead, God has chosen what is foolish in the world to shame the wise, and God has chosen what is weak in the world to shame the strong."[12]

Similarly, if we hope to become discerning people, we're going to have to adjust our understanding of who and what is worthy of honor.

In his first epistle, Peter gives an example of bestowing unexpected honor in the context of marriage. Having instructed wives to honor their husbands regardless of whether they have earned it or not, he now tells husbands, "Likewise, husbands, live with your wives in an understanding way, showing honor to the woman as the weaker vessel, since they are heirs together with you of the grace of life" (3:7 ESV). As we've already noted, every human being deserves honor simply because they are made in God's image.

But Peter's logic is more complicated than this. Peter is teaching husbands to honor their wives *because they are women.*

To understand what Peter is proposing, we must understand how prevailing social values can prevent us from honoring women as we should. If a society honors brute force, a woman's physical vulnerability will immediately mark her as "less than." If a society honors efficiency and wealth production, the nine months it takes her body to create a child will seem wasted. And if a society honors radical individualism, her attention to social inclusion will be an irritant to those eager to move forward regardless of who gets left behind.[13] In such a society, the only way that a woman can achieve honor is by becoming more like a man.

That's why Peter's instructions are so striking. When he commands husbands to live with their wives in understanding, to show them honor because of their vulnerability, he's turning cultural values upside down. He's not calling husbands to condescension or preferential treatment: he's calling them to *particular* treatment. He's calling them to stop engaging their wives as if they were men and to honor their womanhood. He is calling them to get out of their own heads and recognize how very much a woman's experience of the world differs from theirs. In particular, he's calling husbands to understand their wife's unique value.

Peter's logic here is similar to Paul's when he describes how God intends the church to honor the gifts of each member of Christ's Body. "Those parts of the body that are weaker are indispensable," Paul writes in 1 Corinthians, "and those parts of the body that we consider less honorable, we clothe these with greater honor" (12:22–25). The question is not whether men and women are different, but whether we truly honor those differences the way God does. Do we honor women, not just with our words, but with our money, time, and influence? Do we honor their unique perspectives and experiences? Do we honor them, not in spite of their womanhood, but *because* of it?

When we fail to honor those whom God honors, we will miss goodness because we lose access to their unique gifts, capacities, and experiences.[14] But when we extend honor to whom honor is due—regardless of whether surrounding society does—we will find our own value system turned upside down. And when it is, we might be able to benefit from a slightly different perspective.

Honor and Glory

As the story goes, my grandfather asked if he could take *Red Bank* home and was given permission. He wasn't entirely sure what he had found, but he was familiar with Blair and contacted him to see if he wanted his painting back. In his unassuming way, Blair reportedly told him that he was welcome to keep it. After all, Blair said, it wasn't his painting anymore.

Blair's values ran counter to those of the world. When given the opportunity to recover one of his paintings and potentially resell it, he didn't. Instead, he acted with generosity and grace that revealed him to be a man of honor. As we seek "whatever is honorable," we too will often find ourselves running contrary to the values of the world around us. As we learn to honor God's image bearers, we will learn self-respect as well as how to extend respect to others. As we value others for their unique gifts and contributions, we'll be able to benefit from what they can teach us. As we pursue honor, we will become honorable people.

And all of it will point us back to the One who is worthy of honor in the first place.

One of the reasons that God chooses to honor what the world finds unworthy is to ensure that "no one may boast in his presence."[15] By picking the weak and despised, He confirms that He alone—not our talents, wealth, social status, attractiveness, or political power—is the source of our dignity and life. He alone can guide us through this world and assure our eventual glory. So that one day, around His throne in heaven, we will cry with every creature in heaven and on earth and under the earth and in the sea: "Blessing and honor and glory and power be to the one seated on the throne, and to the Lamb, forever and ever!"[16]

Chapter 6

Whatever Is Just

"The line separating good and evil passes not through states, nor between classes, nor between political parties either—but right through every human heart."
—Aleksandr Solzhenitsyn

T HAT'S NOT FAIR! YOU CHEATED!"
When these words reverberate through our house, they're inevitably accompanied by the clatter of tokens being swept off the game board and the bounce, bounce, bouncing of dice across the hardwood floor until they eventually come to rest underneath the couch. When tensions are high, they can also be accompanied by crying and the scuffle of small bodies knocking up against the living room furniture. Fun for the whole family, indeed.

Fighting over board games is a relatively recent phenomenon for us—not because we don't fight, but because we've only recently discovered board games worth fighting over. I realize that many people have warm memories of playing games as children, but for most of my life, I never understood the appeal. Scrabble was interesting in its own way but, surprisingly, one-dimensional. Monopoly was too long and left too much to chance—you might as well just roll the dice at the beginning to see who gets Boardwalk and save yourself three hours. Consequently, I never went out of my way to incorporate board games into our family life. Of course, I'll play them in social settings. I play Rook and Spades for holiday gatherings at my in-laws', submit myself to game night at church, and can manage an adequate level of interest at friends' houses. But if I'm completely honest, a small part of me would die whenever someone asked, "Who wants to play a game?"

And then suddenly, all that changed.

It was the middle of September, and we were heading for a few days of family vacation on Chincoteague, an island off Virginia's Eastern Shore. Chincoteague is relatively quiet, and in the off-season even quieter, so along with the snacks and beach toys, I packed books, puzzles, and a game that I'd bought on a whim. I'd never heard of it before, but a friend had recommended it, and it had something to do with trains, so I thought Nathan and the kids might enjoy it. And in the interest of family fun, I figured I could buck up and endure it, too. The first night, after we'd unpacked and settled in, we got it out, read the directions, and played a round. And then another. The second night we played it again. And again. By the third night, we were staying up all hours playing round after round after round. And I liked it.

Something about this game was different than games I'd played before. The board and pieces were good quality, the artwork appealing, and the game play simultaneously straightforward while still requiring strategy and planning. I enjoyed it so much that I wasn't surprised to later learn it had won the 2004 *Spiel des Jahres* (or German "Game of the Year"). I enjoyed it so much I was thrilled to later learn it belonged to a larger family of board games called Euro or German-style games and that there were many more where it came from.[1] For Christmas, I bought a game based on ancient civilizations; for Easter, a cooperative game in which players save the world from an outbreak of disease. Then I bought an expansion pack for our train game and a game based on the Renaissance jewel trade. Then one with a magical island slowly sinking into the sea and another and another. Today our game shelf is stocked with beautiful, creative games that will guarantee family fights for years to come.

Written on Our Hearts

It usually doesn't take us very long to learn the rules of a new game, and it only takes us infinitesimally longer to determine that someone else is breaking them. As many do, my children have an exceptionally refined sense of the way things should be, an almost trigger instinct for justice. In *The Justice Calling,* authors Bethany Hoang and Kristen Johnson describe this innate logic as the knowledge that something *is not right.* "When we encounter . . . injustice," they write, "we might have a deep, intuitive sense that *this is not the way things are supposed to be.*"[2]

This idea is behind the next virtue that Paul mentions in Philippians 4: "whatever is just." Something is "just" when it fulfills what it is supposed to do, when it is

> SOMETHING is "just" when it fulfills what it is supposed to do.

the way it is supposed to be. Throughout the Scripture, the concept of justice is tied closely to righteousness or, more literally, the "rightness" of something, with God's nature as the standard of what is right. In fact, when God calls us to righteousness, He appeals to His own: "Be holy, because I am holy."[3] This makes sense when you remember that human beings were created to reflect the glory of God. In order for "things to be the way they are supposed to be," we must conduct ourselves in a way that is consistent with His nature—we must act like He acts and do what He does. Surprisingly, our shared identity as image bearers also explains why human beings throughout time and across cultures have held a common understanding of what is just and what is not. Our sense of justice feels innate because it is.

Despite our race, age, religion, or sexual or political identities, despite our personal likes and dislikes, we all have a basic sense of goodness that triggers a "THAT'S NOT FAIR! YOU CHEATED!" response when we suspect someone has trampled on it. This shared value system (sometimes called natural law) explains why human societies inevitably craft laws against murder and adultery, demand respect of elders and fulfillment of family duties, punish dishonesty, and encourage kindness and mercy.[4]

In *The Abolition of Man*, C. S. Lewis notes that this shared sense of justice "is not one among a series of possible systems of value. It is the sole source of all value judgments."[5] So innate is our sense of how things should be that Paul calls it a law "written on their hearts,"[6] which works in tandem with our consciences to point us in the right direction. And Psalm 19 tells us that even the natural world testifies to God's grand design in something as basic as the way the day turns to night and the night turns back to day.

In other words, the way the world is constructed—the way we are constructed—is designed to reveal goodness to us. We can reject our consciences; we can actively pursue things that aren't what they are supposed to be. But at some foundational level, we can all agree that certain things are good. The husband who selflessly cares for his wife when, after a lifetime of marriage, Alzheimer's begins to steal her away from him. The young soldier who sacrifices himself to save his friends. The fragile, unspeakable joy of a baby entering the world. But when goodness is disrupted, we also recognize injustice. We recognize the wrongness of a cheating spouse. We disdain the soldier who betrays his unit. We grieve the loss of miscarriage. We feel the weight of injustice deep within us because the call of goodness is buried deep within us too. And when we're caught by forces that seem outside our control, when we experience injustice, we rage against the world. We cry and scream and flip the board, sending the pieces flying.

Rules of the Game

Still, our general sense that something is unjust is not enough to prove it is not good or to tell us what *is* good. Personal discomfort is definitely not enough, and even natural law is not enough by itself because, in a broken world, how can we tell the difference between what is natural and what is the result of sin? And who's to say which is which? As soon as one of my children declares, "YOU CHEATED!" the other one yells, "NO, I DIDN'T!" and "THAT'S NOT FAIR!" is met with "YES, IT IS!" Such pronouncements are inevitably followed by a rush and flurry and an extraordinarily keen interest in the rule book. Children who could barely sit through its initial reading transform into experts, parsing the finer points of game play, teasing out the logic of an obscure rule, and uncovering the loophole that will validate their claim. (So powerful is the rule book that I once successfully saved the entire world from an outbreak of infection on a mere technicality.[7])

Interestingly, Psalm 19—the same psalm that directs our attention to natural law or general revelation—also directs our attention to how the Scripture reveals what is good in more specific ways. David writes:

> The law of the LORD is perfect,
>   reviving the soul;
> the testimony of the LORD is sure,
>   making wise the simple;
> the precepts of the LORD are right,
>   rejoicing the heart;

the commandment of the LORD is pure,
    enlightening the eyes. (vv. 7–8 ESV)

The words "law," "testimony," "precepts," and "commandment" all refer to God's revealing what is good through the prophets and written Scripture. Notice too how these verses connect the ideas of discernment ("making wise the simple") to Scripture and justice ("the precepts of the LORD are right"). In other words, the Scripture works in connection with our natural sense of justice, refining and illuminating it, in order to teach us what goodness looks like in our life choices.

Despite their sudden interest in the rule book, however, my children aren't primarily interested in goodness; they're interested in self-preservation and winning. They are engaging in self-justifying argumentation that leads only to alienation and isolation.[8] In a board game, the primary purpose of the rule book is to teach you how to play so you can enjoy the game so simply reaching for it in a moment of conflict won't be enough. Similarly, God does not intend us to use Scripture simply as leverage in our arguments with each other. The goal of Scripture is to teach us the best way to play the game.[9] It teaches us how to move our pieces, what our goals should be, and how to interact with other players in a just way.

> GOD DOES NOT intend us to use Scripture simply as leverage in our arguments with each other.

And ultimately, the goal of the written Word of God is to reveal the living Word of God, Jesus Christ. Hebrews explains that while God spoke to people in many different ways throughout history—through nature and the prophets—"in these last days, he has spoken to us by his Son . . . and made the universe through him. The Son is the radiance of God's glory and the exact expression of his nature, sustaining all things by his powerful word" (1:1–3).

Jesus Christ, the logic and power behind nature.

Jesus Christ, the exact image of the Father.

Jesus Christ, the perfect revelation of goodness.

Jesus Christ, the way things are supposed to be.

Jesus did not come to obliterate or overturn previous revelation. He came to fulfill it, to give it full expression in human form, to make sure it does what it is supposed to do—unite us in loving relationship with God and each other.[10] If we want to know what the world should look like, we can't rely on nature or a bureaucratic handling of Scripture. In order to become discerning people, we must embrace Jesus. We must embrace His mission to proclaim "good news" as He did when He stood in the synagogue at Nazareth and read from the scroll:

The Spirit of the Lord is on me,
because he has anointed me
to preach good news to the poor.
He has sent me
to proclaim release to the captives
and recovery of sight to the blind,
to set free the oppressed,
to proclaim the year of the Lord's favor.[11]

Jesus came to make everything what it should be again. He came, as Micah 6:8 says, to do the good that God requires of us, to "act justly, to love faithfulness, and to walk humbly with [Him]." He came as the Creator to restore His broken creation, to show us how things should be and then to make them so.

Because there's nothing quite like watching the maker of the game play it, nothing quite like seeing it played the way it should be played.

Drawing Conclusions

Sometimes we struggle to recognize what is just because we don't understand how natural law, the Scripture, and the revelation of Jesus Christ as God work together. Rather than handling them as a unified whole, we pit them against each other. If we see something in the world that makes natural sense to us, we can easily turn to the Scripture and "see" it there as well, using proof texts to validate it. Or sometimes we'll read a passage in the Old Testament that seems so bizarre that our natural sensibilities tell us that it can't be good, and in order to resolve our discomfort, we uncouple it from the New Testament, declaring that Jesus did away with the Old. Sometimes we even detach Jesus from both natural law and Scripture, interpreting His actions in a vacuum—which, in reality, isn't a vacuum at all but filled with our own preferences and presuppositions.

Practically speaking, how can we know what is just? Does it simply come down to what each of us decides—what we pick and choose?

Despite my antipathy to most games, there was one I enjoyed growing up: *Pictionary*. More often a party game than a board game, to play *Pictionary*, one member of the team draws a picture of an object while the remaining members guess what she is drawing. The game relies as much on the ability to perceive what an object might be as it does on artistic talent. The player might start by drawing a circle and the team will begin to yell out what they think it could be: a ball, the sun, a face, a cookie, a wheel.

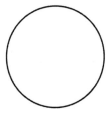

But until the team correctly identifies it, the artist keeps drawing, adding more details.

"A face! A smiley face!" someone blurts out. "It's got to be a smiley face!" The artist shakes her head and keeps drawing.

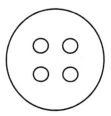

And then someone finally guesses correctly—it's a button.

Here's the fascinating thing: until enough details are in place, the team can't make sense of the original circle. They can see the outline but have no way of knowing whether it's a ball or a cookie or a button; each new addition clarifies what has come before.

The original does not change, but the team's understanding of the original changes. What they once believed to be a ball is really a button, and it has been a button the whole time.[12]

In order to be able to discern what is just—to understand "the way things should be"—we must seek answers that unify all that God has revealed about Himself. We must look for a logic that unites nature, Scripture, and Jesus and be prepared to alter and adjust what we believe about each. If we don't, our "innate" sense of good and bad could potentially lead us in a direction that is completely at odds with Scripture and Jesus Himself. This is particularly important when we're trying to evaluate things that our culture (or even religious subculture) has determined are just or the way things should be.

Because the way things *are* is not necessarily the way things should be.[13]

One example of how our natural sense of justice can conflict with God's sense of justice happens in the realm of competition, leadership, and authority. Within the natural world, we observe a kind of "survival of the fittest"—the strongest animals and plants stay alive and eventually are able to reproduce, passing along their genetic information to the next generation. Within the food web, larger, stronger animals prey on smaller, weaker ones. We see the house cat pounce on the mouse and watch as the lion stalks and devours the gazelle; then we call him the king of the beasts. We understand that there is a certain brutality to nature, accept it as "the way the world works," and celebrate those who can survive.

The problem comes when we have to decide whether or not "the way the world works" is the way the world *should* work. Should the rules that govern animal and plant behavior govern human behavior? If we accept that "might makes right," we will quickly translate it to our interaction with human beings. We will excuse aggression and predatory behavior as normal: the salesman that tacks on hidden fees is simply "smart," and the pastor who berates and pressures his congregation is simply a "good leader." We can also begin to believe that being on top of the heap somehow means that you inherently deserve to be there. After all, in the natural world, the buck with the largest set of antlers is prized because he's been able to elude hunters and predators for years, long enough to grow his 14-point rack. Translating this to human community, wouldn't that mean that folks at the top of the economic, social, and political ladder somehow deserve to be there? And correspondingly, that folks at the bottom somehow deserve to be there as well?

But here is where Scripture adjusts our understanding of what is "natural." The Scripture teaches us that God, and not our own merit, ordains the course of our lives. None of us can control the family we are born into, the education we receive as children, the social function or dysfunction that we inherit. We do not get to pick our IQ, our personalities, or our gifting. We are responsible to steward these gifts, but at the end of the day, God makes some of us mice and some of us lions. And He does this, not as a reward for our ability, but for His own good purposes.[14]

Furthermore, Jesus cautions those with positions of earthly authority to use their influence, not for themselves, but for the good of those under their care. "You know that the rulers of the Gentiles lord it over them, and those in high positions act as tyrants over them," He says in Matthew 20. "It must not be like that among you. On the contrary, whoever wants to become great among you must be your servant, and whoever wants to be first among you must be your slave; just as the Son of Man did not come to be served, but to serve, and to give his life as a ransom for many" (vv. 25–28). It's as if Jesus is asking the lion to protect a lamb. It's as if Jesus is showing the ball to be a button. It's as if He's disrupting the entire game.

Justifier of the Just

The problem with seeking justice is how quickly the process reveals our own injustice. We want the world to be the way it should be only to find that we ourselves are not what we should be. We seek things that are "right" just to realize how not right, how un-right, how unrighteous, we are. But here too, seeking justice leads to goodness, because when we seek justice, we will find the One who justifies the unjust.

Despite the fact that we often know what's right both through Scripture and by our own natural instinct, Paul writes in Romans 3:23 that we all "fall short of the glory of God"—we all are less than what we are supposed to be. But rather than leaving us hopeless, God extends grace to us, offering to make us what we should be through Jesus. "This was to show God's righteousness," Paul explains, "so that he might be just and the justifier of the one who has faith in Jesus."[15]

> WE SEEK THINGS that are "right" just to realize how not right, how un-right, how unrighteous, we are.

In other words, in order to be who *He* is supposed to be, God makes those who bear His image who they are supposed to be.

Through Jesus Christ, we are relieved of the burden of having to prove our goodness, the weight of our rightness resting completely on Him. "For you are saved by grace through faith," Paul writes in Ephesians, "and this is not from yourselves; it is God's gift—not from works, so that no one can boast" (2:8–9). And this is how justice makes us discerning people: when we are no longer troubled with maintaining our own goodness, we can partake of the goodness around us.

This truth is especially important when you realize, after years of playing the game, that you've been playing it wrong—when you realize that what you thought was "natural" is not how the Maker made the game to be played at all. Maybe you're playing with friends when someone lays a card at an unexpected moment or moves their token in an unusual way. "You can't do that!" you blurt out before realizing it. "That's not the way you play the game."

But what if when you reach for the rule book to show someone that they are wrong, you discover—you literally had no idea—that *you* are the one playing the wrong way? What happens when you realize that what you thought was a ball is really a button?

Without God's grace, we will make hapless attempts to justify ourselves and only make things worse. Because we can't risk being wrong, we can't apologize or learn from our mistakes. We lock ourselves into conflict, wasting our time, emotion, and energy trying to defend ourselves. We miss a world of good, beautiful things because we are so worried about making ourselves good and beautiful that we don't have time to see that God has already made us good and beautiful through His Son. And we miss His good gifts because we are too busy trying to earn them.

But when we receive God's goodness, when we humble ourselves and let go of our pride and fear and our need to boast in our achievements, when we recognize that we could never be what we are supposed to be, it opens up an entirely new way of seeing. We can risk looking into the rule book to learn because we can safely entertain the possibility that we might be wrong. But the only way we can entertain *that* is if we don't need to win in the first place. And the only way we can let go of our need to win is if we know that Jesus already won for us. "For indeed, grace is the key to it all," pastor Tim Keller writes. "It is not our lavish good deeds that procure salvation, but God's lavish love and mercy. That is why

THE ONLY way we can let go of our need to win is if we know that Jesus already won for us.

the poor are as acceptable before God as the rich. It is the generosity of God, the freeness of his salvation, that lays the foundation for the society of justice for all."[16]

Just like that, we can see that everything in this life is a gift. Suddenly we can see goodness all around us. And where it is absent, we feel compelled to cultivate it.

Part of God's goal in justifying us is to bring us into His larger work of redemption, of making the world good once again. That's why, immediately after declaring to the Ephesians the free grace of Jesus, Paul continues: "For we are his workmanship, created in Christ Jesus for good works, which God prepared ahead of time for us to do" (2:10). By making us just, God removes the weight of our unrighteousness, relieving us from the need to prove ourselves. And because we no longer have to prove our own goodness, we can focus on what He has called us to do: we can focus on being and doing all that's good.

Let Justice Roll

One reason I like Euro-style games is because they tend to emphasize strategy and player interaction over chance and conflict. While a good game will have elements of both, there's something infuriating about waiting for just the right number to come up on the dice before you can enter play, or worse, being eliminated fifteen minutes into the game. Perhaps games of chance and conflict are more representative of the world as it is, but I like to think that games of strategy and cooperation represent the world as it should be. A world, not of sameness, but of equity and justice. A world where the hand you're dealt doesn't determine whether you get knocked out of the game only to sit on the sidelines. A world where everyone can flourish together.

Ultimately, that's what we're seeking when we seek justice. We're seeking the world as it should be. But as we seek that world, as we pray for the Father's will to be done on earth as it is in heaven, we must never forget that we cannot achieve it in our own strength. Like all good things, this too is a gift of God. On our own, we can never love enough, work hard enough, be smart enough, or have passion enough to set the world right.

But the beauty of God's righteousness is that He holds Himself responsible to make the world just, to make things what they should be. He invites us into that good work and prepares us to become channels of goodness to those around us. The very truth that awakens us to the fact that the world is not as it should be is the same truth that sustains us as we seek justice in it, calling us over and over again to rely on His own righteousness. So that one day, by His grace and power, we will look on the world around us and see it as it should be. One day, we will see the world again made good, just like He said it is.

Chapter 7

Whatever Is Pure

"Praised be You, my Lord, through Brother Fire, through whom You light the night, and he is beautiful and playful and robust and strong." —Francis of Assisi

As the sound of splintering wood echoes through the air, I stop my dinner preparations to look out the window. The dusk is already gathering, but roughly fifty yards away, my husband stands with his arms extended over his head, a splitting maul at the apex of its swing. His hand slides down the wooden shaft as momentum drops the wedge into the log beneath. A loud crack, and the force splits the wood along the grain, sending pieces flying. He bends over to collect them and tosses them into a waiting wheelbarrow. Then he takes another log and places it on the chopping block.

Both Nathan and I grew up in homes heated exclusively by wood, but as adults we've been spoiled by the ease of electric baseboards that come alive with the turn of a dial. No more bare feet on ice-cold floors, no waiting for the wood to catch, no feeding the fire once it does. But having grown up in homes heated exclusively by wood, neither of us can quite give up the draw of a fire. Luckily our house has both an open fireplace and a wood-burning stove. When we use them, we tell ourselves that we're offsetting heating costs, but really, there's something about the earthy intimacy of fire that electric heat can't replace. When I see him splitting wood, I know there is more on his mind than keeping the house warm.

He swings again, but this time the maul lands with a thud and becomes wedged in the wood. Nathan reaches down to free it, wiggling it from side to side. The piles of wood around him— locust, cherry, hickory—have been carefully culled over the previous year. As early as spring and no later than summer, he'll start gathering wood from trees downed by wind, disease, or the concerns of a homeowner and store them in an old lean-to where they season over the next few months. Then when the weather turns cold, and the night is coming on, I'll look up from my kitchen window to see him splitting wood. I watch as he steps up to the log and swings again. This time the maul slices clean through with a satisfying crack. He steps back for a moment to collect his strength, his breath frosty against the encroaching darkness.

There will be a fire in the fireplace tonight.

A Fiery Ring

After calling us to seek whatever is true, honorable, and just, Philippians 4:8 draws our attention to "whatever is pure." Of all the virtues listed here, purity may be the most familiar to us, at least in terms of how it leads to goodness. In the wake of the Sexual Revolution, the church has devoted untold time, money, and energy arguing for the goodness of sexual purity and traditional sexual ethics. We have debated gender roles, sexual identity, and the definition of marriage. We have promoted abstinence, taken purity pledges, adopted the "Billy Graham Rule,"[1] and loudly and legitimately argued that what happens in the privacy of the bedroom has public significance.

But in recent days, this seems to be changing. A 2016 survey conducted by the Public Religion Research Institute revealed that an overwhelming majority of white evangelicals now see less connection between private morality and the common good. While only 61 percent of the general public believes that "an elected official who commits an immoral act in their private life can still behave ethically and fulfill their duties in their public and professional lives," 72 percent of white evangelicals do—a shocking forty-two point jump since 2011.[2]

Pundits have offered many explanations for the shift, but regardless of what caused it, those who once spoke most strongly for the wisdom of purity are now shrugging their shoulders.

Part of the problem may be that, while we have argued for traditional sexual ethics, we haven't always understood how Scripture derives those ethics from a larger understanding of purity. We've learned the rules, but we don't necessarily understand the logic behind them. We don't really understand how faithfulness in our intimate lives predicts and even leads to flourishing in our larger lives. Interestingly, the Scripture uses the image of a fire to explain how purity and goodness go hand in hand.

> WE DON'T really understand how faithfulness in our intimate lives predicts and even leads to flourishing in our larger lives.

Speaking to the priests of the nation of Israel, Malachi prophesies that the Lord was coming as a refiner's fire to "purify the sons of Levi and refine them like gold and silver" (3:3).[3]

This image comes from the ancient art of metallurgy, including the technique of heating ore to a point where the impurities separate from the essential metal.[4] As a result, metal is considered "pure" when it is uncontaminated, when it is the same substance throughout and unmixed with anything else. That's why, in common usage, the word pure can describe everything from gold to essential oils to water. Being pure is the condition of being whole and untainted.

When Malachi tells the priests about the Lord's coming, they push back, demanding that he explain why the Lord is angry with them. "Because," Malachi responds, "even though the LORD has been a witness between you and the wife of your youth, you have acted treacherously against her. She was your marriage partner and your wife by covenant" (2:14).

The Lord was coming to purify the priests of their infidelity. They had made promises to their wives and failed to keep them. They had said one thing with their mouths and done something different with their bodies. They were not whole. But the priests' adultery was symptomatic of a larger duplicity. They had also been unfaithful to their callings as priests. "The lips of a priest should guard knowledge . . . " Malachi tells them. But, "You, on the other hand, have turned from the way. You have caused many to stumble by your instruction" (2:7–8).

The priests' unfaithfulness to both their wives and their work revealed them to be unfaithful men to the core. In this sense, their adultery did not make them impure; they committed adultery because they were already impure.[5] They had divided hearts.

This nuance helps us understand why the Scripture uses sexual ethics as shorthand for a larger life of purity and faithfulness. The danger of immorality is not simply that we have crossed physical lines. The choices we make sexually reveal our heart's posture toward God and each other. Are we so divided that we will take all the privileges of sex without the responsibilities of commitment? Are we so defiled that we will love ourselves first and foremost *in the very act of lovemaking?*

This is why the covenant promises of marriage are foundational to Christian morality. The promises we make to each other are the basis on which we call each other to love and self-sacrifice. And whether we fulfill our promises to those

THE CHOICES we make sexually reveal our heart's posture toward God and each other.

closest to us predicts whether we will fulfill our promises to the broader community. A man who cheats on his wife will cheat those under his care elsewhere. A woman who cheats on her husband will cheat her customers in the marketplace. And a priest or pastor who is unfaithful to his marriage vows will be unfaithful to his ordination vows.[6]

Ultimately, Malachi tells the priests the root of their unfaithfulness is their fractured hearts: "You ask, 'How have we wearied [the LORD]?' When you say, 'Everyone who does what is evil is good in the LORD's sight, and he is delighted with them'" (2:17). In other words, the priest's adultery was symptomatic of how their entire moral framework had already been turned upside down; they lacked the wisdom and integrity to call good "good" and evil "evil." And when this happens, you can justify just about any form of impurity.

It was this deeper impurity that God was coming to purify. He was coming to purify them of their divided hearts and tainted motives so they could love Him with their *whole* heart, soul, mind, and strength, and their closest neighbor as themselves.

Candlelight

I can hear Nathan piling the logs near the back door, the dull thud of wood knocking against the brick. We have to run down to Small Brick Church for a bit after we eat, but he'll have everything ready for when we return. I finish readying dinner and call over my shoulder, "Kids! Come to the table!" knowing that it will take more than this for them to come. While I wait, I busy myself with taking plates and glasses out of the cupboard and counting out silverware. It's silent outside now; I glance out the window to see Nathan pushing the wheelbarrow back to the woodshed. He'll be in soon.

I try again, "Time for dinner!"

My daughter wanders into the kitchen, and I immediately send her back out. "Go tell your brothers that I said 'It's time for dinner.'"

She turns and yells, "Boys! Mommy sa—"

"I said *go*."

I hear the creak of the basement door as it opens and the rattling of glass as it shuts. Heavy footsteps on the stairs tell me that Nathan is inside and headed upstairs. Moments later, the sound of footsteps charging down the hall tell me the boys are on their way too. They burst into the kitchen, a flurry of arms and legs and a strange mix of giggles and protests. The eleven-year-old races to the table and grabs the pillar candle that sits in the middle of it.

"Mommy, can I light the candle, where are the matches? Mommy— Mommy, can I light the candle? Phoebe did it yesterday; I get to light it today." Distracted by the last details of dinner, I don't answer. He takes this as permission and goes in search of the matches himself, impatient to strike a flame.

One reason that Paul calls us to seek purity is because the stakes of impurity are very high. When we confuse passion for love, we have the potential to wreak havoc on ourselves, those closest to us, as well as those we profess to love.[7] Knowing this, and the ease with which we are tempted, can lead us to set strict boundaries to protect ourselves and those we love from it. We guard what they watch, where they go, and who they spend time with—as well we should. After all, one of the best ways to keep a child from playing with matches is to simply keep the matches out of reach. But what happens when he finds them? What happens when no one is around and he discovers matches for the first time?

One of the mistakes that we can make in pursuing purity is to assume that naïveté or ignorance is the same as discernment. But having never encountered evil is not the same as knowing the difference between good and evil or knowing what to do when you do encounter it. Quite the opposite, the Scripture suggests that naïveté can actually lead to impurity because simple people, as Proverbs calls them, are primed to be manipulated.

Distinguishing them from fools (those who actively embrace evil), the "simple" are at risk because they can't identify evil in the first place. Unlike the prudent who "sees danger and takes cover," naïve people never see it coming.[8] That's why one of the primary goals of Proverbs is "teaching shrewdness to the inexperienced"[9] so that they won't be misled by impure men and women. One of the main examples of simplicity in Proverbs happens in the context of sexual purity when a naïve young man is seduced by a married woman. "She seduces him with her persistent pleading. . . . He follows her impulsively like an ox going to the slaughter . . . he doesn't know it will cost him his life."[10] But as much as naïve men are at risk to predatory women, naïve women are at risk to predatory men and perhaps more so.

In 2006, activist and sexual assault survivor Tarana Burke coined the phrase "Me Too" as part of an initiative to help young women of color who had been victims of sexual violence. The phrase picked up unexpected momentum in the fall of 2017 when actress Ashley Judd leveled accusations of assault and sexual harassment against Harvey Weinstein, one of Hollywood's most powerful producers. Within days, other women came forward with similar accounts of abuse, including Alyssa Milano. She retweeted the following and suggested others who were victims of sexual harassment or assault reply with "me too":

Me too.

Suggested by a friend: "If all the women who have been sexually harassed or assaulted wrote 'Me too' as a status, we might give people a sense of the magnitude of the problem."[11]

The tweet went viral, unleashing a flood of stories that crossed racial, socioeconomic, geographic, religious, and political boundaries. In its wake, Hollywood moguls, politicians, academics, entertainers, and even church leaders were exposed as sexual predators.[12] Like any movement, the #metoo movement is highly politicized and easily leveraged for private agendas—by both progressives and conservatives—but if there's one takeaway that we can all agree on, it's that the world is still a dangerous place for women and girls despite the promised freedom of the Sexual Revolution. Maybe it's even a *more* dangerous place.

Wise to What Is Good

While it's true that men *should* behave honorably toward women, that they should respect their physical autonomy and their no, the reality is that women need the force of community and the legal system to hold immature and selfish men to the responsibilities that come with sex. But when the Sexual Revolution positioned sex as a personal and private matter rather than something to be safeguarded in community, it created an ethos that privileges untamed male sexuality. Even worse, the decline in marriage, the hook-up culture, and widespread pornography have shaped the world in which both our sons and daughters live and how they understand sex itself. In a long-form essay in *The New York Times*,[13] Maggie Jones cites a 2016 study[14] in which teenagers reported that pornography was their primary source for information about sex—more than friends, siblings, schools, or parents. "There's nowhere else to learn about sex," one boy told Jones. "And porn stars know what they are doing."

Jones's findings underscore a principle that Proverbs teaches about the naïve. The reason naïve people are so easily misled is because they are ignorant. Because they don't know what evil looks like, they also don't know what good looks like. In their ignorance, they are gullible, believing whatever people tell them. In the context of sexuality, they are gullible enough to believe that the violent, aberrant sex of pornography is how mature people engage in intimacy.

> THE SOLUTION to impurity is not simply abstinence or ignorance; it is to pursue whatever is pure.

Given the epidemic we're facing, it would be natural to quarantine everything related to sex, to speak in hushed, guarded tones, to opt out of sex education, to strictly guard our interaction with the opposite gender. But given the epidemic, it's likely that we need to speak more about sex, not less—to talk about it more frequently and sooner. And we need to speak about it in ways that affirm the holiness and celebrate the beauty of our God-given sexuality. The solution to impurity is not simply abstinence or ignorance; it is to pursue whatever is pure.

In discussing how to protect the church from false teachers, Paul clarifies the difference between purity and naïveté:

> Now I urge you, brothers and sisters, to watch out for those who create divisions and obstacles contrary to the teaching that you learned. Avoid them, because such people do not serve our Lord Christ but their own appetites. They deceive the hearts of the unsuspecting with smooth talk and flattering words.[15]

Like Solomon does in Proverbs, Paul calls the believers to recognize that there are people in this world actively trying to trick and mislead them, sometimes even using Christian language to do it. They are con men and abusers, and we must guard against them. But the way we guard against them is not to ignore them; it's to actively draw our attention to them and accept that they exist, even in our own churches and communities.

Paul continues: "The report of your obedience has reached everyone. Therefore I rejoice over you, but I want you to be wise about what is good, and yet innocent about what is evil." To understand the distinction Paul is making between purity and naïveté, we must understand that ignorance is not the same as spiritual formation. We become innocent of evil, not by preserving ignorance, but *by becoming wise about what is good.* We become innocent of evil by learning to have no part in it: to be uncontaminated, unmixed, and pure. In other words, the best way to preserve someone's innocence is to show them the difference between good and evil and teach them how to pursue whatever is pure—to invite them to walk with us in our own pursuit of purity: to be open and honest with the struggles, to celebrate the joy and security of lifelong commitment, to delight in the God-given goodness of our physical bodies.

Because here's the unsettling reality: simply having never been exposed to evil does not ensure that a person will choose good when given the opportunity. Simply learning to not touch the matches will not keep our children safe. We must teach them to use them properly.

When my son moves to find the matches, I stop what I'm doing and get them down for him. I follow him to the table and remind him of how to safely handle a match. I watch as he takes one out of the box and slides it closed again. His fingers grip it too tightly and his hands shake a bit. When he tries to strike it, it breaks. He gets another one and tries again. This time the match bursts into flame. I can see the wonder in his eyes, the feeling of power that comes from holding fire in your hand. But there's fear too, and he begins to move too quickly to keep from burning his fingers. He fumbles and struggles to light the wick; I put my hand on his shoulder. He relaxes, and then succeeds.

The Pure in Heart

I was six years old when our house was struck by lightning and caught fire. We were out of state visiting family when it happened, and at the edges of my memory, I remember my parents getting the call and my knowing that something serious had happened. I remember my father leaving us to assess the damage while we stayed with family. But surprisingly, I don't remember feeling unsafe. The next three years we lived with my grandmother felt more like a gift; and the years we spent building a new house on the spot where the old one had burned, an adventure.

As an adult, I realize that my parents experienced those years differently. They spent the next decade recovering, and everything for them was marked by whether it happened before or after the fire. The things that did survive were water damaged and, even years later, carried the unmistakable smell of smoke. Oddly enough, when my parents rebuilt, they decided to heat with wood and placed a cast-iron woodstove in the very center of the house. Today, I marvel at this. I marvel at the fact that after all they experienced they could ever trust fire again.

I marvel too that once we experience sexual brokenness and the danger of impurity we could ever trust sex again. That we could ever trust each other again. That we could ever believe that goodness could be in any way associated with sexuality's fiery power.

But as much emphasis as the Scripture places on pursuing purity, it places equal if not more emphasis on being purified. Because the truth is that none of us, as hard as we try, are pure. As we judge things against the standard of God's whole and holy faithfulness, we quickly see how far human beings fall short. As we examine our own actions, beliefs, and motives, we very quickly see the deceitfulness of them. "Who can say 'I have kept my heart pure; I am cleansed from my sin'?"[16]

We can't. But as we see our own unfaithfulness, we'll begin to entrust ourselves to the One who is faithful. And when we see God in all His purity and faithfulness, we will melt like gold and silver in a refiner's fire. No secret sins, no lack of integrity, no hidden desires can withstand Him. No shame, no taint, no corrosion can remain. Standing before Him, our impurities are removed and we are made whole. For when He appears in a bright blaze of purifying fire, "we will be like him because we will see him as he is."[17]

> As WE SEE our own unfaithfulness, we'll begin to entrust ourselves to the One who is faithful.

And to those of us who submit to the purifying process, God

promises to preserve us—to make sure that we pass *through* the fire instead of being consumed by it. So that:

> When through fiery trials thy pathway shall lie,
> [His] grace, all sufficient, shall be thy supply;
> The flame will not hurt thee; [He] only design[s]
> Thy dross to consume and thy gold to refine.[18]

Fire Light

Outside it is dark. The fields surrounding Small Brick Church are empty, the cows having long been shuttered in barns, but just beyond the fields, where the woods thicken and the darkness deepens, predators lie in wait. But tonight, in the warm shadows of the sanctuary, we will pass a flame to each other, slowly filling the darkness with light. We begin to sing, as if our voices alone could hold back the night.

"Silent night, holy night; All is calm, all is bright . . ."

I watch my children, each with their own thin white candle, proud of the opportunity to hold a live flame. They move and jostle and wiggle, and the light from the wick jumps with each movement. I worry that they will extinguish it or, worse, that they'll catch themselves on fire. Proverbs asks whether a man can carry a fire next to his chest without burning his clothes,[19] and I wonder too whether a child can hold a candle in the sanctuary of the congregation and not burn us all to ashes.

"Round yon virgin mother and child; Holy Infant, so tender and mild . . ."

I reach out to steady the youngest only to feel the drip of wax on my own hand. I've tilted my candle too far; the wax runs off the cardboard skirt onto my flesh. For a moment it burns and then hardens.

In Philippians 1, Paul prays that the believers' love would abound with all knowledge and all discernment so that they would be pure and blameless.[20] This is my prayer for my children too. I pray that their love may abound. That they will know the goodness of pure intimacy. That they will have the wisdom to be blameless. That in the darkness, their little light will neither flicker out nor set them on fire. That they will seek whatever is pure.

We make it through the service unharmed, wish each other well, and return home where a fire waits for us. After tucking the children in, my husband and I sit in front of it, watching the flames leap and twist off the wood. He reaches out to touch my hand, and we decide against putting another log on. We stand and head to bed where we sleep together in heavenly peace. We sleep in heavenly peace.

Chapter 8

Whatever Is Lovely

"We want something else which can hardly be put into words—to be united with the beauty we see, to pass into it, to receive it into ourselves." —C. S. Lewis

I have worn the same pair of earrings almost every day for the last ten years. Every night, I take them out and lay them on the table next to my bed. Every morning, I pick them up again and place them in my ears. I haven't worn them uninterrupted—occasionally, I've opted for dangling costume jewelry, hoops that match a necklace, or glass beads that catch the light. But barring special occasions, I have worn a pair of 8mm cultured pearls that Nathan brought home from a trip to Japan.

They came to me in a bright yellow bag bearing the words:

Pearls, Wally Yonamine, 7-14-8, Roppongi, Minato-Ku, Tokyo

But how they came *there*, I'll never know. I'm also not entirely sure how a man who grew up in a one-stoplight town in Appalachia came to ascend a staircase in one of Tokyo's wealthiest districts and enter a boutique whose clients have included Henry Kissinger, Willie Mays, Elizabeth Taylor, Isaac Stern, Yo-Yo Ma, and Barbara

Bush. The immediate route was clear enough. Nathan had gone to visit a college buddy, whose work in the US Army stationed him just outside Tokyo. Ever the adventure-lover and perpetual instigator of experiences, his friend guided Nathan to the Great Buddha of Kamakura, Hiroshima, and the Tsukiji Fish Market, where they walked through stall after stall offering up the bounty of the neighboring sea.

At some point, they visited Yonamine Pearls, and upon entering the shop, Nathan was immediately greeted by ropes and ropes of pearls. Pearls set in platinum rings and encrusted with diamonds. Pendant pearls hanging from 18K white gold chains. Half-shell shaped brooches with a flawless pearl in the center. He just as quickly realized that almost everything was out of reach for a young pastor with a wife and three children. But then, he spotted a pair of simple pearl studs; they lay in a blue velvet box, elegant, understated, and perhaps a bit less out of reach. Within minutes, they were wrapped and placed in the bright yellow bag to make their 6,600-mile journey home to my earlobes.

Those Shining Pearls

Nathan is not the first man to succumb to the loveliness of pearls. In an eighth-century Japanese love poem, a traveling husband writes:

> How I wish to send home to my love
> A package of those lucent pearls,
> That she might string them together
> With orange-blossoms and sweet flag flowers!
>
> O for the abalone pearls
> They dive for, I hear,

Crossing over to the holy isle of the sea!
I would pack and send them home.

O for the lucent pearls
From the holy isle of the sea,
That I might send them to my love
To comfort her heart!

How happy should I be,
Were there a fisher-maid to give me
Those shining pearls by the hundred.
Scooping them up in her hands![1]

The "fisher-maid" that the poet refers to are the *ama*—women who for millennia have free dived deep into the ocean, drawn down, down, down in search of seaweed, clams, urchins, and the abalone, who hide pearls within themselves. Passed down from mother to daughter, the work of these "women of the sea" is part of the larger culture of Japanese coastal villages. While their fishermen husbands and fathers wait in boats at the surface, the *ama* plunge into the ocean's icy depths, sometimes as deep as thirty feet, and swim free, aided by nothing other than a broad knife and basket with which to bring their treasures to the surface again.[2]

So perhaps neither man nor woman can resist the loveliness of a pearl.

After calling us to pursue things that are pure, Paul calls us to "whatever is lovely"—to seek and think about things that are worth being loved.[3] Related to the ideas of beauty and goodness, the word translated "lovely" appears only this once in the New Testament and comes from a combination of two Greek words, *prós* and *philéo*, that communicate the experience of being drawn toward something out of pleasure or desire for it. To describe

MORE THAN drawing us to themselves, beautiful things draw us *beyond* themselves to a greater reality.

something as lovely, then, is to describe both the thing itself as well as the response it produces in us.

Lovely things have a kind of gravitation that pulls us toward them. So when we encounter the loveliness of pearls, we stop. We gaze. We wonder. And we move toward them in order to join with them. We dive deep to find them. We reach out to buy them. We pick them up to put them in our ears.

But more than drawing us to themselves, beautiful things draw us *beyond* themselves to a reality greater than either of us. "Beauty . . . prompts a search for a precedent," Harvard professor Elaine Scarry explains. "The mind keeps tripping backward until it at last reaches something that has no precedent, which may very well be the immortal."[4]

Don't get lost in Scarry's language. What she's describing is what we all experience when we stand in front of a rushing waterfall and catch our breath; what we experience when we look up into the night sky and gaze in wonder at the constellations; what we experience when we bring a sprig of lilac to our nose and inhale. If anything, we know the experience of beauty too well to understand it—its draw is far too natural and too immediate for us to even recognize what's happening. We know what David means when he sings that "the heavens declare the glory of God, and the expanse proclaims the work of his hands."[5]

We may not be able to put it into words, but we know this experience. We know what it feels like to be drawn outside ourselves to the eternal, the majestic, the sacred, and the glorious. We know how beauty can stop us in our tracks, interrupt our fixation with the mundane, and remind us that there is a world beyond the one in front of us. We know how "beauty can pierce the heart, wounding us with the transcendent glory of God."[6]

The power of beautiful things to draw us to a reality beyond the present is why art has always been a significant part of religious communities. From God's detailed instructions for the Tabernacle to majestic soaring cathedrals to the simple handcrafted beauty of a mountaintop chapel, these spaces are designed to do more than house the congregation. They are intended to draw worshipers up and out of themselves toward heaven. That's why in John's vision of the New Jerusalem, he foresees a city resplendent in beauty—gold, fine jewels, lush gardens, flowing rivers, and, yes, even pearls: "The twelve gates are twelve pearls; each individual gate was made of a single pearl. The main street of the city was pure gold, transparent as glass."[7]

Kingdom of Heaven

For most of human history, pearls were hunted from the bottom of the seas and waterways, but the pearls we buy today—the pearls that are currently in my ears—are pearls that have been cultivated and harvested on farms. By the late 1800s, overharvesting had depleted sources of natural pearls, making them increasingly rare and expensive. Seeing an opportunity, the enterprising Kokichi Mikimoto began experimenting with the possibility of "growing" pearls; by implanting an irritant into an oyster, he could trigger it to respond and secrete a liquid (nacre) that solidifies in layer upon layer.

Mikimoto hired local *ama* to collect abalone from the seabed so he could culture them; the ama then returned them to sheltered areas or beds. In 1893, after multiple failed attempts and brushes with bankruptcy, Mikimoto succeeded in producing the world's first cultured pearl, opening the way for people everywhere to enjoy their beauty. "My dream," he once said, "is to adorn the necks of all women around the world with pearls."[8] Today, the house of Mikimoto, with its shops in London, Paris, and New York, is synonymous with luxury.

In Matthew 13:45–46, Jesus tells the story of another pearl merchant who comes across a pearl of rare quality and brilliance. Unlike Mikimoto pearls, this pearl is a natural, or wild, pearl that only one in ten thousand oysters produces. The merchant is fixated. Not only is it rare, it's exquisite—its luster unlike any he's ever seen. When the light strikes it, the reflection is so sharp he imagines he can see his face in it. It's so large and round that there's no telling how long it sat on the ocean floor being slowly formed, layer by layer. And now, here it is in his hands. He must have it. So the merchant returns home, gathers all his worldly goods, and sells them so he can buy it.

With this parable, Jesus is illustrating the level of commitment and sacrifice necessary to possess the kingdom of heaven—a level of commitment and sacrifice few of us have ever seen. The closest we might come to understanding it is the draw we feel toward something lovely and valuable like a pearl. Because besides hinting to a world beyond the present one, lovely things also teach us that good things are worth sacrificing for. That despite their cost, good things are necessary.

Here is the risk if we do not seek whatever is lovely: If we do not learn how to let lovely things draw us to sacrifice to possess them, we will never understand why Christ was willing to sacrifice everything He had for us. If the pearl represents the kingdom of heaven, then the merchant represents the One who sacrificed all He had to buy it.

In John 3:16, Jesus tells us of how God's love for the world has drawn Him to it: "For God so loved the world," He declares, "that he gave his only begotten Son, that whosoever believeth in him should not perish, but have everlasting life" (KJV). While Jesus is testifying to the vast love of the Father, He's also pointing to the fact that God loved the world. Just as He did at creation, God looked at the world and declared it worth loving.[9] He looked on the world and declared it worth redeeming. Even if it meant sending His Son from the glories of heaven to sacrifice for it.

It's hard to see what God found lovely in us. It is a mystery to us the same way lovers cannot fathom why the other loves them, why they whisper in hushed tones about the marvelous kindness of such a gift. But they do, and He does, and so we do too.

We find Him lovely because He first found us lovely.

We find Him beautiful because He first declared us beautiful.

We are drawn to Him because He first allowed Himself to be drawn to us.

We find Him worth sacrificing for because He first sacrificed Himself for us.

We will sell all that we have to find Him because He left all that He had to find us.

Counting the Cost

As much as beauty draws us to things beyond ourselves and teaches us that good things are worth sacrificing for, it also turns our understanding of sacrifice on its head by teaching us that what the world considers "sensible" isn't necessarily wise. *Because how exactly do you put dollars and cents to the longing you feel when you read a book? How exactly do you quantify the value of flowers and the time it takes to smell them? How can you justify bringing home pearl earrings from faraway places?*

In a broken world, we often define goodness as whatever produces a result by the fastest, most efficient means possible—regardless of whether it leads to long-term happiness. After all, when you're struggling to survive, who has time for lovely things? When you struggle to pay the bills, who can afford niceties?

I remember facing this dilemma on an almost daily basis as a young mother. As lovely as they are themselves, infants and toddlers are time and soul consuming.[10] So in the midst of the diapers and feedings and doctor's appointments, it became easy for me to neglect my own care—things like showering. And fixing my hair. Putting on make-up. Dressing in clothes that made me feel lovely. Instead, I would choose to do more quantifiably productive things like laundry or making a grocery list. I prioritized activities that had a direct, clear function and moved me toward an objective, while neglecting anything that required me to slow down, to stop in wonder, to gaze, or to be drawn out and up the way beauty does.

In many ways, this utilitarian mindset was the mindset of the rich young ruler who came to Jesus in Matthew 19. When Christ called him to sell all he had to follow Him, the young man balked. It simply didn't make sense. He wasn't opposed to hard work; after all, he had kept all the law and he had come to Jesus to specifically ask Him the way to eternal life. But when Jesus asked him to love and value the kingdom of heaven the way the merchant valued the pearl—to sell all for it—the numbers didn't add up. And so he turned away from the loveliness of Christ and went home.

Like it did for the rich young ruler, a utilitarian mindset has the potential to lock us into the horizontal plane by convincing us that physical reality is ultimate, the survival of our physical life most important. Such a mindset does not understand the need to sacrifice for beautiful, lovely things. Such a mindset could potentially arrive in heaven and wonder why God spent so much money on streets of gold when asphalt would have done just as well.

Such a utilitarian mindset could keep us out of heaven entirely.

As the rich young man leaves, Jesus turns to His disciples and warns them that "it will be hard for a rich person to enter the kingdom of heaven" (19:23). The problem is not our riches, but a mindset that lets the bottom line define what is good and what isn't. In such a value system, beauty cannot compete. In such a value system, we cannot see the worth of something that is slow and unpredictable and unquantifiable. And if we let the desire for money keep us from sacrificing for beauty in this life, that same mindset most certainly has the potential to keep us from experiencing it in the next.

A few years after Nathan returned from Japan with pearls for my ears, we found ourselves unable to make ends meet. He was unemployed and then underemployed. We were on food stamps and our children on Medicaid. I remember questioning how we had spent our money and whether we had been good stewards, and, surely, if we just buckled down and worked harder, we'd be able to get back on our feet. And yet, the whole time I walked around with pearl earrings in my ears and never once thought about selling them.

I didn't sell my earrings because I couldn't afford to. Beautiful things were especially important to me in those days— my earrings, my wedding ring, a bouquet of flowers, a good meal—because they reminded me of deeper realities beyond my present difficulties. Just as I would not spend money I did not have, I would not sell what I *did* have because it was far too valuable.

UTILITARIANISM becomes a threat to discernment when it teaches us to evaluate what is good and bad by earthly definitions of value.

Ultimately, utilitarianism becomes a threat to discernment when it teaches us to evaluate what is good and bad by earthly definitions of value. And when this happens, our churches become finely oiled machines with little room for beauty; our public witness is reduced to pragmatic political agendas; and our interpersonal relationships means to ends. When we embrace a utilitarian mindset, what Mark Noll describes as "dominated by the urgencies of the moment,"[11] there is the possibility that we will miss the values of an *eternal* God.

The power of lovely things is that they turn our value systems on their heads and point us to greater realities. When we sacrifice for what is lovely, we begin to understand that it's not simply what has the highest price tag. When we pursue things of true beauty, we learn that what is truly beautiful is the inner person. And when we seek what God loves, we know that it is not charm but those who fear Him.[12]

Siren Call

Once we are convinced that lovely things are worth pursuing, we still face the challenge of knowing what is truly lovely. Simply because we are drawn to something does not mean that it is worth pursuing. After all, doesn't the search for purity teach us that our hearts are deceitful and desperately wicked? How can we trust our own desires?

In the fourth century, Augustine, a bishop in North Africa, pondered these same questions and suggested that the problem isn't that we love things that we shouldn't, but that we love what we should in the wrong way. Our sense of beauty isn't wrong, but we're not allowing beauty to do what it's supposed to do: draw us to love God more fully and to love our neighbor as ourselves. The fact that we can respond wrongly to beauty helps us understand the tension between attraction and lust.

One of the difficulties of pursuing whatever is lovely is that the people around us are very lovely beings, and we don't always know how to relate to their loveliness in discerning ways. Because beauty draws us to itself, we can quickly confuse natural beauty or attraction for permission to indulge in inappropriate thoughts and relationships. As if hearing the call of the Sirens of ancient mythology, we feel powerless to resist another person's wit, charm, physicality, or even kindness. We rightly see them as beautiful (because what image bearer isn't?), and we succumb. And when we do, we can begin to blame the beautiful object instead of our disordered desire.

There was something so lovely, so attractive, so compelling about her body that I was powerless. He saw me and knew me and took interest in me—what else could I do?

But once we realize how easily our desires escape us, there is also the real risk that we would dismiss and ignore the loveliness of another person. Because we don't trust ourselves to respond to them appropriately, we hold them at arm's length, effectively resisting and denying their loveliness. But in denying the things that make them lovely—their wit, kindness, experience, strength, or intelligence—we find that we are unable to love them for who they are, for who God has made them to be. And being unable to love them rightly, we also find that we can't love God rightly either.

But here's where a proper understanding of beauty helps us: beauty calls us to goodness beyond itself. Beauty calls us to sacrifice for that good. Beauty calls us to turn our values upside down.

A woman or man can be an object of our admiration. We can feel drawn to them. We can recognize and identify their wit or beauty or desirability and still relate to them in ways that are holy and good. The word "lovely" in Philippians 4 is based on the

Greek root for the love between brothers and sisters: *phileō*. And this is exactly how we must engage the loveliness that rests on each other. We must engage each other as brothers and sisters who are seeking each other's good.[13] We must let each other's beauty draw us heavenward.

So when we truly see the loveliness of our brothers and sisters, our hearts will respond as it does to any other form of loveliness: in celebration of their Creator—a Creator so wise, so imaginative, so kind as to create each one of us. And when we celebrate their Creator, we will guard the loveliness He has made. We will sacrifice for it, even if it means sacrificing our own desire for it. This is something of what we mean when we talk about not objectifying other people. Their beauty is not ours to possess; it is not ours to consume. It is ours to protect.

Today, there are only about two thousand *ama* left in Japan. Despite age and dwindling numbers, they continue their traditional work of foraging the sea's bounty, still diving without a breathing apparatus, often well into their 70s. In a 2017 interview, lifelong fisherman Masumi Nakamura of the Ise-Shima region speaks with pride of his sixty-four-year-old wife: "Sayuri is the best and fastest *ama* out there." He adds, "My number one condition when marrying was that the woman be an *ama* diver. This way we could spend our days together."[14]

Of the challenges facing the *ama*, the greatest comes from deciding whether and how far to adapt their traditional profession to the modern world. After all, if they used oxygen tanks, they could stay under water much longer than the one, possibly two, minutes they do now. For that matter, why even dive? Surely there are technologies that can cull the seabed without risking life and limb. But being an *ama* is more than a profession; it is a way of life. A way of life that is integral to both family and community. And so for the time being, the *ama* continue to dive, carrying on the traditions of their mothers and grandmothers before them.

The idea that we should pursue what is lovely and train ourselves to respond rightly to it may seem as old-fashioned as the ways of the *ama*. But when I look at the superficiality and general ugliness of the world around me, I wonder why we've waited so long and whether we can wait any longer.

WHEN WE seek whatever is lovely, we are drawn to the One who is altogether lovely.

For when we seek whatever is lovely, we are lifted above the paltry urgencies of this life and given a vision of the next. When we seek whatever is lovely, we are drawn to the One who is altogether lovely and begin to understand why the Father calls Him "Beloved." We begin to long for Him the way lovers long for each other:

> So long have I not seen you
> Whom I long to see like the white pearls:
> I scarcely feel alive,
> Remaining in this distant land.[15]

Then like the *ama*, we find ourselves diving deeper and deeper in search of Him, leaving behind lesser things. We find His goodness binding our hearts to Him, drawing us on, ever pursuing, ever seeking, ever searching until the beauty of the Lord finally rests upon us.

Chapter 9

Whatever Is Commendable

"I probably shouldn't say this, but . . ." —Everyone

Steam billows from an electric kettle as I reach up into my cupboard to retrieve a couple coffee cups. For a moment, my hand hovers in front of the second shelf as I consider which ones to grab. They're an odd cast of characters: there are the ones gifted by Sunday school children, the one celebrating my role as a pastor's wife, and the one I got from the Christmas gift exchange three years ago. Behind those are the mugs I've schlepped home from conferences and retreats, branded swag whose primary purpose for existence is to remind me that certain organizations exist.

A few years ago, when I thought it was important to have matching dinnerware, I bought a set of nondescript cups and saucers from a Scandinavian home goods store. They sit high on the third shelf, just enough out of reach to be only worth bringing down for company. Next to them are a set of clear glass mugs purchased when I'd become fixated on specialty hot chocolates and frothed coffees, the ones garnished with dollops of real whipped cream and finished with a peppermint stick or sprig of mint. Both sets seem resigned to their lot in life, patiently waiting as if more aware of my tendencies than I am.

My favorite, though, is a ceramic mug of the functional variety that populates small town diners, greasy spoons, and hole-in-the-wall eateries. Mine comes from the now defunct Blue Ridge Restaurant, Inc., in Floyd, Virginia, whose official address (according to the logo emblazoned on the front) is "Across from the Courthouse." As mugs go, it's not a very good mug. The lip is too wide, the gap between the cup and handle too narrow, and it only holds enough coffee to ensure that a waitress will earn her tip by regularly stopping by to refresh it.

But today I need a different mug. I need one wide enough and deep enough to carry me through a conversation. I glance over at my friend Jess, who is sitting at my kitchen table waiting for me to complete my paces. No, I need two. I select a pair that will work and place them on the counter in front of me. As the kettle reaches the right temperature, a subtle click cuts the power supply. I lift it to pour the steaming water into the French press. As I do, I say, "I don't know if you've heard . . ."

And with that it begins.

A Good Word

For the next hour or so, we'll devote ourselves to conversation, our hands wrapped around warm mugs, our bodies leaning across the table as we share what we've learned and are learning. We'll sit back and laugh at the latest community drama and shake our heads and sigh, wondering how we'll ever survive parenting and marriage. At some point, I'll get up to refresh our coffee or wander to the pantry to see if I can scrounge up some forgotten cookies. We'll joke that my kitchen table is free therapy for both of us. And each time, I'm struck by how an invitation to "come on over for a cup of coffee" is so much more than that.

Having established the importance of lovely things, Paul next calls us to pursue whatever is commendable and uses a word that only appears in the New Testament twice: *euphēmos*.[1] Some translators have chosen to render it as things "of good report" or "of good repute," but the idea is larger than simply pursuing things that get good reviews or have popular appeal. *Euphēmos* literally means "speaking well" and refers to speech that is thoughtful, appropriate, considered, and careful. In his use of the same word in 2 Corinthians 6:8, for example, Paul contrasts *euphēmos* with slander; but you might be more familiar with another of its antonyms, *blasphemous*. When someone blasphemes, they denigrate or speak inappropriately about things that deserve honor and respect, including things of a religious or sacred nature. In his commentary on Philippians, New Testament professor Matthew Harmon addresses the complexity of *euphēmos*, noting that "this word often referred to speech that demonstrated cautious reserve or was carefully chosen."[2]

By extension then, seeking whatever is "commendable" means giving attention to both what we talk about and how we talk about it. Becoming discerning people includes developing a taste for things that *should* be communicated and avoiding things that are best left unsaid or unuttered. It's understanding that what a person chooses to talk about reveals as much about them as what they say about it. It's knowing that what we give attention to will shape us and the world in which we live. It's aligning ourselves with people who speak well and becoming those people ourselves.

In many ways, seeking whatever is commendable is tied to the discipline of rhetoric. Ancient Greek philosophers like Plato and Aristotle developed theories about public speaking, many of which are the foundation for our modern understanding of how human beings communicate with each other. The Roman rhetorician Quintilian, a contemporary of Paul, defined rhetoric as "the art of speaking well" or a "good man speaking well."[3] In its most basic sense, rhetoric examines what, why, and how we speak with each other. It studies all the choices we make in communicating an idea—whether we frame it positively or negatively, what aspects we choose to highlight, what types of words and phrases we use, and the credibility of the speaker. It also investigates what makes an idea persuasive to someone or which ideas will be successful in certain spaces—why one message may resonate with one group but fall flat with another.

Today, the field of rhetoric is highly developed, and professionals work in a variety of applications including corporate communications, public relations, academia, marketing, and politics. But at some level, we all are rhetoricians. We are all curators, collectors, and exhibitors of information. The stories we find important, the jokes we tell, the things we feel are essential to get off our chest—all of these things reveal our deeper motives, fears, and beliefs. And whether we share it on Facebook or over a cup of coffee, every one of us adds to and shapes the culture around us, the culture that we then live in. As author Annie Dillard observes, "How we spend our days is, of course, how we spend our lives. What we do with this hour, and that one, is what we are doing."[4] So too how we spend our words is, of course, how we spend our lives.

If we spend our days sharing trivialities, life will be trivial. If we spend our days focused on what we fear, life will be filled with anxiety. If, however, we spend our days talking about good, worthy, glorious things, there is the

> IF, HOWEVER, we spend our days talking about good, worthy, glorious things, there is the strong likelihood that our lives will be filled with good, worthy, glorious things.

strong likelihood that our lives will be filled with good, worthy, glorious things. In this sense, the call to whatever is commendable supersedes Greco-Roman categories and taps into a larger, more universal truth—one as ancient as the foundation of the world itself: words and ideas have power. With words, God spoke life into existence. With words, the Scripture reveals truth. And as the Word made flesh, Jesus Christ dwelt among us.

Shop Talk

The ritual Jess and I enjoy—conversation around a cup of steaming caffeine—has a long history that began in the Middle East and spread slowly west. The first coffeehouses in England opened in the late 1650s and were initially a curiosity—a place to sample this exotic black liquid. But proximity to universities in Oxford and to businesses in London quickly made coffeehouses a gathering place for exchanging information. During its heyday in the seventeenth and eighteenth centuries, the coffeehouse was decidedly egalitarian, at least in terms of class and wealth.

The seventeenth-century poet Samuel Butler described them as having "no distinction of persons, but gentleman, mechanic, lord, and scoundrel mix." This patronage resulted in what he described as "a kind of *Athenian* school, where all manner of opinions are profest and maintain'd to the last drop of coffee."[5]

In other words, everybody got together to talk about everything, and the caffeine in the coffee kept them going.

So effective were coffeehouses at facilitating the sharing of information that they became referred to as "penny universities," where for the price of a cup of coffee, a patron could gain access to all kinds of conversations regardless of his standing in broader society. From medical advice to scientific discoveries to economic and political theory, the coffeehouse played an essential part in equalizing knowledge.

Of course, these more noble conversations happened alongside the gossip and heated argumentation that naturally accompanies any gathering of more than one person. Because of this, coffeehouse culture was not without its detractors. Some worried that the social dimension discouraged serious study and distracted students from the rigors of the university. Others believed that coffeehouses would become hotbeds of political insurrection and promote religious nonconformity. So concerned was King Charles II that in 1675, he attempted to close them down, citing that "the great resort of Idle and disaffected persons to them, have produced very evil and dangerous effects . . . but also, for that in such Houses . . . divers False, Halitious[6] and Scandalous Reports are devised and spread abroad, to the Defamation of His Majestie's Government." He insisted that purveyors stop selling "any Coffee, Chocolet, Sherbett or Tea, as they will answer the contrary at their utmost perils."[7]

Not surprisingly, given the addictive properties of coffee, the proclamation met fierce resistance and never took effect.

Today, social media functions in many of the same ways that the coffeehouse did during those centuries. Both allow for unprecedented access to information and unprecedented ability to share that information. Conversations are no longer governed by established institutions like the academy or church. With few boundaries, speech is freer, livelier, and more powerful. While this has benefited many (myself included), it comes with the responsibility to wield it appropriately. Because we are literally creating data in real time, we must exercise greater care in what we choose to add to the conversation and how we react to what others contribute. More than ever, we must develop the discernment that recognizes that not every shared idea is a good idea, nor is every idea that we have worth sharing.

This is especially difficult in a world that begs for us to be constantly posting, constantly tweeting, and constantly adding information to our communal knowledge base. Retweets, comments, likes, and shares reward us for sharing information regardless of what type of information it is. In fact, a recent study by researchers at the Massachusetts Institute of Technology suggests that this emotional reward actually propels the spread of false information.

Analyzing data from over 136,000 Twitter cascades from 2006 to 2017, researchers determined that false news travels six times faster than true news and that human beings are mostly to blame for this. Researchers think that both the novelty of being the first person to share news (and thus not wait for confirmation) as well as the deep emotional reaction that false news stories tend to generate causes us to share them at a rate higher than even robots do. "We saw a different emotional profile for false news and true news," Soroush Vosoughi, coauthor of the study, explained in an *MIT News* article. "People respond to false news more with surprise and disgust."[8]

And it's precisely this emotional reaction that seeking whatever is *euphēmos* keeps in check. If we pursue what is commendable, we will have to pause long enough to weigh our responses, to consider whether what we're about to share measures up. Instead of simply clicking a button or swiping the screen to move information through our

> IF WE PURSUE what is commendable, we will have to pause long enough to weigh our responses, to consider whether what we're about to share measures up.

circles of friends and followers, we will have to pause to determine whether it should have been shared with us in the first place. We have to ask ourselves whether it meets the basic standards of truth, honor, justice, purity, and beauty.

In other words, giving attention to whether what we say is "commendable" forces us to take responsibility for what we contribute to the broader conversation. Because once we share something, not only is it impossible to take back, we've altered the body of information that shapes our culture and community. This is part of why Proverbs cautions us that "death and life are in the power of the tongue" (18:21).

But giving attention to *euphēmos* also forces us to take responsibility for our own hearts because the words we speak and what we choose to share reveals who we are. "How can you speak good things when you are evil?" Jesus asks the Pharisees.

> "For the mouth speaks from the overflow of the heart. A good person produces good things from his storeroom of good, and an evil person produces evil things from his storeroom of evil. I tell you that on the day of judgment people will have to account for every careless word they speak. For by your words you will be acquitted, and by your words you will be condemned."[9]

Polite Conversation

As terrifying as it is to think that we will give account for our words (especially in the digital age), Jesus also makes a salient point about the positive power of words that are *commendable*. Words that are wisely chosen have the power to build up other people and create a larger culture of goodness. Just as coffeehouses gave social outsiders access to ideas, sharing good information can have an exponentially positive effect as well. "A word spoken at the right time," Proverbs says, "is like gold apples in silver settings" (25:11). Good speech, true words, and beautiful stories have the power to give people life.

But sorting through whether something is good and worth sharing is no easy task, especially when what is good is not comfortable or "nice." Should we share a point of constructive criticism with a friend? Is it wise to post your perspective on a hotly debated political issue on social media—or would that somehow damage your public witness? In the face of complex or uncomfortable conversations, we often choose to bypass the dilemma altogether. We either tell little white lies or go mute, having been trained that if we can't say anything nice, it's best to not say anything at all. But when the Scripture calls us to whatever is commendable, it is calling us to something greater than niceness—it's calling us to speak what is right and good. It is calling us to speech that is richer and more robust than either platitudes or silence. Remember that discernment is not concerned primarily with our social comfort. It is concerned with goodness. And sometimes pursuing goodness will lead us outside the boundaries of polite conversation.

To appreciate the complexity of this, consider Paul's instructions to the Christians at Ephesus. After establishing core doctrines like salvation by grace, he turns his attention to how these truths work out in daily life. In chapter 5, he explores the nature of Christian communication and tells them to refrain from "obscene and foolish talking or crude joking," which "are not suitable, but rather [to give] thanks" (v. 4). It's easy to understand how this injunction fits with the call to pursue whatever is commendable. But then things get complicated only a few verses later.

> For you were once darkness, but now you are light in the Lord. Live as children of light—for the fruit of the light consists of all goodness, righteousness, and truth—testing what is pleasing to

the Lord. Don't participate in the fruitless works of darkness, but instead expose them. For it is shameful even to mention what is done by them in secret. Everything exposed by the light is made visible. (Eph. 5:8–13)

On the surface, it appears that Paul is talking out of both sides of his mouth. Because we are children of light, we are to expose the unfruitful works of darkness. But it's shameful to speak about the sinful things that people do in secret. *How are we supposed to expose the evil while simultaneously not speaking about it?*

Just as in Philippians 4:8, Paul's goal is not simply to tell us which topics to speak about but to teach us how we should speak about them. Are our words *euphēmos*? Or *blasphemous*? Do we glorify things that deserve shame? Do we shame things that deserve glory? When Paul writes that it is shameful even to speak of things done in secret, he is not putting a gag order on exposing hidden sins[10] or limiting us to a certain set of socially acceptable topics. Once again, he's emphasizing that what we choose to speak about and *how* we speak about it are part of the message we send to each other and the larger culture we create. We must consider and give *appropriate* weight to each topic. If we don't—if we speak lightly about serious things, and seriously about inconsequential things—we will be unable to discern what is good because our entire moral ballast will shift.[11]

> WHAT WE choose to speak about and *how* we speak about it are part of the message we send to each other and the larger culture we create.

Paul's primary concern in this passage is that children of light should not align themselves with darkness. One way that we might do this is by talking about evil in an approving way. We can laugh or joke or even glorify it. But we can also participate in evil by silence or by diminishing the severity of it. When we simply won't speak against evil—whether because we have a vested interest in maintaining status quo or because we're preserving our own sense of comfort—we enable it to continue. When we refuse to expose the things done in secret, when we are silent in the face of wrongdoing, we become party to it by the simple fact that we have done nothing to stop it. As Holocaust survivor and Nobel Prize winner Elie Wiesel observes, "Neutrality helps the oppressor, never the victim. Silence encourages the tormentor, never the tormented."[12]

Instead of encouraging silence, Paul calls us to use our words to expose evil, to literally call it out. As much as seeking whatever is commendable compels us to speak appropriately about what is good, it also calls us to speak appropriately about what is bad. And the only appropriate way to speak about evil is to call it by its name.

In Good Company

Even as coffeehouses flourished in Western Europe, women were not welcome in them because established mores viewed the coffeehouse as a public and, thus, male-dominated space. But this did not keep women from holding court in their own spheres of influence. If the academy and coffeehouse belonged to men, the dining room and front parlor belonged to women. By literally controlling who could have a seat at the table, socially conscious women used their role as hostesses to facilitate important conversations and decide which topics gained traction under their roofs.[13] In France, the sitting rooms of wealthy women became so influential that the *salon* became synonymous with a place of refined dialog and exchange of ideas.

But such influence was not reserved for elites. Across the

Channel in eighteenth-century England, some middle-class women began leveraging their homes to introduce and promote radical ideas like prison reform, animal welfare, and the abolition of slavery.[14] In 1792, one of the more dramatic initiatives struck the very heart of British social life: teatime.

To draw attention to the evils of slavery and force Parliament to act, British abolitionists boycotted the sugar that was produced on slave plantations in the West Indies. Calling it "blood-stained sugar," women led the boycott from their pantries. Within months, merchants reported a drop in sales of West Indian sugar and a corresponding rise in sales of sugar from other areas of the world that did not utilize slave labor. But not everyone was a fan of the disruption. Opponents claimed that women were acting out of mere sentimentality and sparked robust conversations about the nature of femininity.

In response to critics, an abolitionist paper in Bristol published an anonymous poem that mocked the moral complacency of those who professed disgust at slavery but refused to disrupt social norms:

I own I am shock'd at the purchase of slaves,
And fear those who buy them and sell them are knaves;
What I hear of their hardships, their tortures and groans,
Is almost enough to draw pity from stones.

I pity them greatly, but I must be mum,
For how could we do without sugar and rum?
Especially sugar, so needful we see;
What? give up our desserts, our coffee, and tea![15]

Suddenly teatime—what was supposed to be a time of polite conversation and gentility—had become the center of a heated, public debate. And it was because women decided to use their voices to expose the unfruitful works of darkness—despite living in a time when their voices could not be heard in the academy, Parliament, or even coffeehouses. For the sake of conscience, they spoke where they could, even if it was only from their own kitchens and parlors.

At the same time, speaking against evil does not give us a *carte blanche* to speak in any way we choose. Discernment is about learning to speak well. When we choose to pursue what is *euphēmos,* it includes guarding our own heart against temptation. We must be sure not to speak in a way that titillates our own sinful desire. As much as we must not avoid uncomfortable conversations, we must not take delight in them either. We do not take delight in displaying our righteousness or in recounting salacious details. Instead, speaking whatever is *euphēmos* includes feeling the weight of sin and speaking about it with a corresponding gravity. Even as we bring evil to light, we must "live as children of light."

> As MUCH AS we must not avoid uncomfortable conversations, we must not take delight in them either.

Because this is always the larger goal: We pursue speaking rightly so that the oppressed would be set free, but we also pursue speaking rightly so those who walk in darkness might awaken to their own danger, that those participating in unfruitful works would be made alive to good works. With Paul in Ephesians 5, we call out to them, "Awake, O sleeper, and arise from the dead, and Christ will shine on you!" (v. 14 ESV). Awake and rise to the morning sun.

Good News

Most mornings, Nathan makes me coffee. Before I stumble out of bed, barely conscious, the remnant of dreams hovering on the periphery of my thoughts, he will already have gotten up and flipped on the electric kettle. When I finally emerge, there on the kitchen table next to a plate of eggs will be a mug and a French press of steaming coffee. Usually, it's only been eight hours since I've last talked to him, but I find that I still have so much to say. So many thoughts, so many ideas, so many things that came into clarity through the night. But not yet.

First I must say good morning and thank you and how did you sleep. Before I bombard him with information, I must first speak well to him.

What we choose to communicate and how we choose to communicate has profound implications on whether we find the goodness we're seeking in this life. With our mouths, we can tear down or build up. We can confuse or clarify, share cynicism or hope. And just like the God in whose image we're made, we can illuminate the darkness with a word of good, good news. Perhaps that's why the prophet Isaiah sings,

How beautiful on the mountains
are the feet of the herald,
who proclaims peace,
who brings news of good things,
who proclaims salvation,
who says to Zion, "Your God reigns!"[16]

How beautiful indeed.

III

———————

"... if there is any moral excellence and
if there is anything praiseworthy—dwell
on these things. Do what you have learned
and received and heard from me, and seen
in me, and the God of peace will be with you."

—PHILIPPIANS 4:8—9

Chapter 10

Every Good Gift

"Learning to see precious things is an acquired skill. It starts with the realization that what may at first be apparent is not necessarily so." —Maxwell L. Anderson

The smell is unmistakable and hits you as soon as you walk through the door. It's not exactly unpleasant, but it is distinct: the smell of mothballs and dust, of worn textiles and decaying books. It's the smell of time and humanity and a hundred thousand different lives assembled in one place. It's the smell of the thrift store.

Many people don't like the smell—I do my best to remove it from my purchases too—but in the right place and at the right time, I find it oddly appealing. To me, it smells of possibility and discovery. Here, you might find a cut glass candy dish that looks exactly like the one your grandmother had or a midcentury vinyl footstool that fits perfectly in your midcentury brick ranch or a metal flashlight that makes you feel like Nancy Drew when you use it. As I stroll through the aisles, I wonder, *How did this get here? And that? What circuitous route brought you and me together in this same place at this same moment? I know how I got here, but how did you?*

I see a platter and wonder whether a young housewife received it as a wedding gift. Or did she purchase it on a whim one day and then decide she didn't like it the next? I touch the sleeve of a man's tweed jacket and think about how nobody dresses up anymore. Did the previous owner worry about that too? Three uncomfortable office chairs lie tossed on top of a dented metal desk—did they land here because of an office renovation or a bankruptcy? How many years did that jewelry box, with its velvet lining and gold clasp, sit on a woman's dresser? When did the child decide she was done with dolls and allow her mother to send them away?

I suppose the eclectic nature of thrift stores can be unsettling, even disorienting, for some people. There's no predictable supply, no reliable order, no telling what you'll find or even what you're looking at. When you spot the left shoe of a pair of vintage Florsheim wingtips in the men's section, you might need to search in the women's section for the right. And there's no such thing as a coming round for a second look; once you see something, you have to put it in your cart immediately. Time and Goodwill wait for no man.

You also have to relinquish the expectation of finding something in particular. You cannot simply wake up one morning and decide to buy a dozen pewter mint julep cups, the ones with beadwork around the top and bottom, and that your absolute limit is $2 a piece and then just pop down to The Salvation Army to pick them up. That's not how thrifting works. But if you're lucky enough, if you're out and about at just the right moment, you might stumble across them like I did one afternoon.

In many ways, life offers up its dilemmas and opportunities with about as much predictability as a thrift store offers up used goods. Sure, we may plan and prepare and predict, but at the end of the day, we have very little control over the chances we're given and the questions we face: *Should I take this job? Is this school the right one for my children? What's the next step for my life?* All presume you are in a position to have a job, you have children, and you will continue to live. When we finally come to a decision, we make it in one moment in time, but that moment came to us through our previous decisions, the decisions of the people who came before us, and the power of God to weave them together in a way that suits His purposes.[1]

Because we can't custom order our lives, we must become people who can spot goodness wherever and whenever we encounter it. Perhaps the randomness of life is also why Paul calls us to think about *whatever* is pure, honorable, just, pure, lovely, and commendable and why he repeats this idea in the final phrase of Philippians 4:8: "if there is any moral excellence, and if there is anything praiseworthy—dwell on these things." Rather than introduce another virtue, this phrase summarizes the previous ideas, bringing the verse to a crescendo: If there is *anything, anywhere* that is true, honorable, just, pure, lovely and commendable; *whatever* you can find that is excellent and praiseworthy; *wherever* you find it—focus your mind and attention on these things.

But Paul's call to seek "whatever" and "anything" is not a wholesale embrace of all the world offers; it is a conditioned one. Because quite frankly, a lot of things the world offers are junk, broken beyond repair, and you'd be foolish to take them home. Instead, Paul impresses on us the need to glean or sort through the mess so that we don't miss what *is* good. He is particularly emphasizing this point because when we walk into the thrift store, smell the smells, and see the chaos, there's a good chance that we'll

> PAUL IMPRESSES on us the need to glean or sort through the mess so that we don't miss what *is* good.

walk right out again. But if you stay, if you sort through the mess, you might find yourself coming home with treasure.

Good Taste

Over the years, I've learned that the trick to buying clothes from Goodwill, or anything really, is to figure out how to not dress like you buy your clothes from Goodwill. But as I told Nathan recently, the line between a wardrobe that is vintage and eccentric and one that is outdated and tacky is fine, and I'm not always sure I'm on the right side of it. Successful thrifting really depends on the eye of the purchaser—whether she has developed an instinct for what's worth buying and what's best left on the shelf. So as much as I enjoy thrift stores, I can't say that I enjoy taking my kids with me because they're still developing this instinct, and more often than not we end up arguing about whether to buy a sparkly owl pencil case that's obviously outlived its usefulness.

When I do take them with me, we always have a conversation on the way. As I'm pulling onto the highway, I'll look in the rearview mirror, make eye contact, and say: "Alright, everybody, let's go over The Rules." They know immediately what I'm talking about. To give structure to our shopping, I've developed three questions about potential purchases:

1. Is it in good condition?
2. Is it worth the price?
3. Did you talk to me about it?

With these questions, I'm hoping to minimize the possibility that I'll find myself standing in the back of Goodwill arguing about a pencil case, but I'm also hoping to help my children develop their instinct for what is good and what isn't. Because a thrift store is unpredictable and full of temptations, I can't rely on a list of what to buy and what not to buy. With my luck, as soon as I ban sparkly owl pencil cases, they would find a sparkly unicorn one. So instead of making specific policies to cover every possible scenario, I'm trying to give my children *principles* that cover many different ones.

In much the same way, the various virtues Paul gives us in Philippians are principles to help us figure out whether something is good. Because we will encounter so many different things in this life, we can't rely on lists or specific boundaries; we can't say "do this" or "don't do that." There are simply too many opportunities, too many unique situations, and too many sparkly owl pencil cases in the world. So instead, these virtues act as a type of shorthand—principles we can apply to *whatever* life may bring. And as we apply these principles, they develop our "taste" for goodness, simultaneously guiding and shaping us.

Nobel Prize winner Joseph Brodsky explains this concept, as it relates to reading, in a lecture he delivered at a book fair in Turin, Italy, in 1988. Speaking to the crowd, he addresses one of the greatest challenges they face: There are simply too many books and too little time. How can you know what you should read? Giving time to one book means you can't read another. Worse still, some books are good and others aren't—if you spend time reading a bad book, you won't be able to read a good one. So how can we know what books we should read without actually reading all of them?

Brodsky notes that we could rely on other people to tell us what to read, but with hundreds of thousands of books published each year, even if we trusted other people's opinions, collective wisdom couldn't keep up. Instead, Brodsky says that we must develop the skill to know whether a book is worth reading within a few pages. And how do we do that? By reading poetry.

Brodsky argues that poetry is "the most concise, the most condensed way of conveying the human experience."[2] By reading it, you will learn what good literature looks like in a shorter amount of time. You learn about the importance of detail, word choice, layering, allusion, and anticlimax. And then you can transfer this knowledge to prose, enabling you to decide whether a book is worth continuing or whether you should put it aside.[3] "All I am trying to do," he tells his audience, "is to be practical and spare your eyesight and brain cells a lot of useless printed matter."

And what Paul is trying to do by turning our attention to the principles of virtue is to provide a similar approach to navigating the world around us. There's poetry to virtue that trains us to recognize goodness in an efficient way, which is particularly important given the number of decisions we face every day. Interestingly too, when the Scripture teaches us how to apply virtue, it also uses poetry. All of Scripture will help us become wise, but certain sections of it are focused more directly on developing our ability to apply wisdom in daily practice. Theologians call these books "Wisdom Literature," and they are generally comprised of Job, Psalms, Proverbs, Ecclesiastes, and Song of Solomon.[4]

Written predominantly in poetry, these books initially appear to lack cohesion or overarching logic. They vary from the deeply personal to the pragmatic; one minute they're praising God and the next, they're questioning Him. They offer beautiful, soul-stirring language right next to prosaic advice about parenting.

In a classic case of form following function, wisdom literature (and particularly the book of Proverbs) is about as diverse and random as our daily lives. We face questions about work and family while simultaneously sorting through friendships at the same time that we're wrestling with our finances. But rather than give us specific answers, the Bible gives us poetry. It gives us test cases and story problems and examples of what it might look like to apply discernment, helping move from the theoretical to the practical. Brodsky suggests that a couple months immersed in poetry can help you develop a sense of what's good in literature, and I'd suggest that a couple months immersed in the poetry of Proverbs or Ecclesiastes could do the same for our sense of what's good in the world at large.

The Enemy of the Good

As I'm learning to identify what's good in a thrift store, I start out by rejecting anything that never had intrinsic value to begin with, things that were poor quality the day they left the factory: off-brand toys, cheaply made furniture, trashy novels, etc. When I see something that looks promising, I check for any obvious signs of wear that would keep it from fulfilling its purpose—rips, stains, and broken or missing pieces. But this is where it starts to get tricky. Determining whether something is in "good condition" can be hard when everything is second-hand to begin with. *Can a scuff mark on a pair of leather shoes be removed? Does a scratch on the side of a coffee table make it unusable? How much wear and tear is acceptable?* I won't settle for less than goodness, but I also understand that I'm shopping at a thrift store so I don't expect to find perfection either.

In the same way, existing in a broken world affects our search for goodness and our ability to exercise discernment. During His earthly ministry, Jesus told a parable to illustrate this dilemma. As the story goes, a farmer planted a field of good grain, but during the night, an enemy came and secretly planted weeds in it. For weeks, the weeds and grain grew together undetected. Eventually as the grain and weeds matured, the field hands discovered what happened and prepared to pull the weeds. The farmer stopped them, saying that pulling the weeds would only uproot the wheat. Instead, he told them to wait until harvest and separate them then.[5]

For whatever reason, God has decided that it is best for us to live in a world where wheat and tares grow side by side. We know that a harvest is coming, but for the moment we exist in the "already, not yet"—that time between sowing and reaping. This doesn't mean we accept brokenness as good, but it does mean we accept the difference between goodness and perfection. That's why Paul's language of "whatever" and "if . . . anything" is helpful. Behind his advice is the assumption that the world is not as it should be. So in order to embrace "whatever" and "if . . . anything," we must learn how to make choices in a broken context. We must learn the difference between unprincipled pragmatism and principled pragmatism.

> To EMBRACE "whatever" and "if . . . anything," we must learn how to make choices in a broken context.

For some, pragmatism is a four-letter word that means making decisions based on "whatever works" regardless of whether it is good or not. Maybe your boss asks you to "rearrange" a few figures in order to help a client cover up a budget shortfall. If you do, he promises, you'll prove yourself loyal and be next in line for a promotion. It'd be easy to rationalize—after all, your boss is the one asking you to alter the numbers. Don't you have a responsibility to follow his instructions? And you certainly could use the extra income . . . maybe this is God's way of providing. And so you compromise. Sure you don't like it, but that's the way things get done.

In its neutral form, however, pragmatism does not necessarily mean compromising ethical principles to reach a certain goal; it simply means giving attention to the practical realities that surround a decision, seeing the various dimensions of the situation, including its practical limits. Surprisingly the Scripture encourages certain forms of pragmatism. It warns against accepting bribes, but it also advises that giving a gift often smooths the way.[6] A judge should not be unjust, but because they often are, the persistent plea, like that of the widow in Luke 18, can be effective. And in a bit of advice that seems out of character, Jesus speaks favorably of the shrewdness of an unjust servant and encourages His followers to use earthly wealth to build relationships of eternal value.[7]

What Scripture objects to is *unprincipled* pragmatism: making choices that take advantage of the brokenness and perpetuate it. While principled pragmatism factors the brokenness of this world into decision making, *unprincipled* pragmatism factors out the reality of both judgment and redemption.

Unprincipled pragmatism will happily sacrifice virtue for temporary gain. It forgets that not only will we one day have to give an account to God for changing the figures in the company books, but that there will likely be a reckoning here on earth too. It assumes that our sins won't be found out, that we can safely cut ethical corners and not pay the consequences. Unprincipled pragmatism does not weigh the risk to other people who will be affected by our actions—the employees who will lose their jobs when the company collapses under criminal investigation; the shareholders whose life savings suddenly evaporate; friends and family who will endure public shame with us. In other words, unprincipled pragmatism doesn't remember that the harvest will come.

What this means for discernment is that we must always operate with an eye to both our present brokenness and our ever-present redemption. We must be humble enough to accept our inability to make a perfect decision, but we must also accept how readily our hearts will exchange virtue for something we want in the moment. Because as often as we make good decisions, we also find ourselves making poor ones on impulse, motivated by a deeper fear, anger, scarcity, and pride. As often as I have made good, well-thought-out purchases from thrift stores, I also bought that chair that sat in my basement for two years until my husband sent it to the trash; that necklace I thought might be pearls only to discover that they were glass beads; and those dozens of cheap, plastic toys that have cycled through my house. So too, I have made wrong choices in my spiritual life; I have sinned against God and against others. I have harmed myself and those I love. I have been foolish and unwise. But even here virtue will guide us if we let it.

When we make a poor decision:

Truth enables us to face it and speak honestly about it;
Honor reassures us that our worth does not rest on our good choices;
Justice leads us to repent, receive forgiveness, and move toward repairing the situation;
Purity teaches us to reflect on why our heart made the choice in the first place;
Loveliness reminds us that good things are worth the sacrifice; and
Euphēmos guides us to confess our mistakes to each other so that we grow.

The possibility (probability) of making a mistake has the power to paralyze us. Not wanting to ever misstep, we set up strict guidelines and fence upon fence. But most of the time, we are not trying to protect ourselves from bad decisions as much as we are trying to protect ourselves from the punishment we've learned comes with missstepping. But if our choices are being driven by fear instead of faith, they are wrong regardless of whether we ever step outside the boundaries or not.[8] Instead of being paralyzed by the possibility of making mistakes, we must learn to trust the goodness of God—to trust that even if we do fail, even when we do make a mistake, His goodness will lead us to repentance and bring us safely home.[9]

Willing to Pay

If I find something that is in good condition, the next step is to evaluate whether it is worth the price. For the most part, thrift store items are relatively inexpensive, but when I'm considering the cost of something, I consider more than the amount of money I'd pay to own it. I also consider the time it would require to refurbish it, the space it would take up in my house, and the emotion and attention it would consume. Something can be generally good and also not worth what it would cost me personally.

And here's where I make a bit of a confession: I have a hard time leaving a "good deal" at the store.

Whether it's a thrift shop, the clearance corner at the grocery store, or the paint aisle at Lowe's, I regularly return home with things that I didn't intend to purchase. I once bought a five-gallon bucket of gray paint for the sheer fact that it was 75 percent off. Then there was the time I picked up fifteen jars of canned yellow tomatoes because they were 19 cents and had been grown and shipped from Italy (to be fair, the label was also very pretty). And last month, I came home with twenty packages of Jell-O because they were on quick sale.

For some of us, saying no to good things can be just as hard as saying no to bad things—especially if you have lacked goodness in your life in the past. When you finally experience goodness, it is simultaneously wonderful and anxiety inducing. As much as you enjoy it, you simply can't trust it. A history of poverty—whether financial, emotional, relational, or spiritual—tells you that you can't trust goodness to last, and if it does, something bad is probably lurking right around the corner. This scarcity mindset can sometimes lead to a type of stockpiling, endlessly seeking good experiences, good relationships, good ideas, and good things to feel secure.

But it is entirely possible to have too many good things, and part of discernment includes trusting God enough to be selective about the things we take into our lives. Paul develops this idea in 1 Corinthians 6 when he responds to the suggestion that our liberty in Christ means that we can partake of everything we want: "'Everything is permissible for me,' but not everything is beneficial. 'Everything is permissible for me,' but I will not be mastered by anything" (v. 12). Paul's concern is not whether something is objectively good or not, but whether it is good *for him*—whether it furthers the work God is doing in his life or hinders it. Commenting on this passage, James Montgomery Boice writes, "The guiding principle here is whether you as a Christian are using things or whether things are using you . . . [things] can control the person instead of the person controlling [them]."[10]

At some point, everything we take into our lives—good or bad—has a cost. Whether it's engaging in a particular ministry, enrolling our kids in afterschool activities, taking on new work assignments, or starting or ending a relationship, all of these things require something of us. In order to discern whether something is worth that price, we must have a clear sense of what God is calling us to and what He is not; we also must trust that He's working everything in our lives for good. This foundation gives us the clarity we need to align our decisions with the work that He's already doing—even if that means saying no to good things.

For me, this means seeking God through prayer, getting perspective from spiritual counselors, and identifying the clear signs of providence in my life, i.e., do minor details, opportunities, gifts, and timing seem to align, leading me toward a certain choice? I also ask myself the following questions:

Does this opportunity fit my specific calling, or could anyone do it? *Should* someone else do it?

Can I justify the time, effort, and energy? Is the exchange fair to everyone, especially to those who are closest to me?

Do the people near me sense God calling me to this opportunity? Would I be disobedient to say no?

Would I be saying yes for wrong reasons, like people pleasing, fear of missing out, greed, pride, or celebrity?

Would I be saying no for wrong reasons, like laziness, insecurity, timidity, or fear of responsibility?

"Discernment," C. H. Spurgeon once quipped, "is not knowing the difference between right and wrong, it is the difference between right and almost right."[11] Tweaking that ever so slightly, discernment is knowing the difference between what is good and what is better. And sometimes, seeking what is better means learning to trust God while you wait for Him to supply it.

One way I'm learning to say no to good, but not necessary, things is by cultivating a mindset of abundance, remembering that God is the giver of all good gifts. Even if I don't take the opportunity in front of me, God will still provide for me; His love and goodness was never dependent on my making the right choices in the first place. If His providence provided this opportunity, it can provide another. As in

> EVEN IF I don't take the opportunity in front of me, God will still provide for me.

Philippians 4:19, my God shall supply all my needs in Christ Jesus, and because He will, I can be content. I can trust Him enough to walk away from good things because I know that there is no shortage of goodness in His world, and as a good, good Father, He will provide for His children.

Look and See

Even as I'm learning the skills necessary for successful thrifting, I'm still trying to teach them to my kids. Just because they can recite The Rules back to me doesn't mean that they've learned how to use them in real life. I still need to stand in the aisle and talk through the process with them. I need to remind them of what goodness looks like and point them to better choices. And through it, I hope I'm helping them develop the maturity to bypass what is not worth buying in favor of what is—how to examine, how to have a critical eye, how to discern, all until it becomes natural to them.

In a 2017 documentary on the life of farmer and writer Wendell Berry, daughter Mary explains how Berry and his wife Tanya guided their children through life this same way:

> We were told to look and see. . . . That field was plowed incorrectly. Why is that? What should have been done? That man is a great farmer. See what he does? That is beautiful. Look and see that it's beautiful. And that's ugly – that's a scar. Look and see that.[12]

This kind of engagement echoes Moses's words to Israel in Deuteronomy 6:

> "Love the Lord your God with all your heart, with all your soul, and with all your strength. These words that I am giving you

today are to be in your heart. Repeat them to your children. Talk about them when you sit in your house and when you walk along the road, when you lie down and when you get up." (vv. 5–7)

Somehow in the doing is the becoming. Somehow in the teaching is the learning. Somehow in the seeking is the finding. So too, it is by the *practice* of discernment that we actually become discerning people. You'll never learn discernment until you start to apply it. You'll never begin to understand the difference between good and bad and good and better until you do it. But as you do, as you seek all that is true, honorable, just, pure, lovely, and commendable, you'll move from a place of not knowing what goodness looks like to finding it almost effortlessly.[13] And soon you'll see it everywhere.

Lost and Found

My home is full of things I've gleaned from thrifting. Our kitchen table where we gather to eat. The matching lamps that light our family room. A small corner cabinet that I bought for $3, painted red, and still makes me happy just to look at it. The dresser in our bedroom and the jewelry box that sits on top of it. A clock that I also painted red. The copper kettle on my woodstove. The chair I sit on as I write this. Pictures, art work, records, hats, glassware, books—a world of treasure and curiosity.

I think what I love most about thrifting is that, in some small way, it feels like an act of redemption. David writes in Psalm 113:7 that God "raises the poor from the dust and lifts the needy from the trash heap," which sounds a lot like thrifting to me: something that was no longer wanted, thrown to the side, and deemed of no value is suddenly given new life. It's not a perfect metaphor, of course, but there's something there, I think. Not only have my thrift store finds been saved from destruction, they also have been made useful once again. They don't simply sit in my house—they do what they were created for. They have purpose.

So I can't help but feel a particular affinity to these lost and found objects, these reminders of grace and goodness. And I can't help but think that the work of cultivating discernment is part of the larger work that God is doing in the world. A work of rescue and redemption, of recovery and restoration. The work of making all things good once again.

Chapter 11

Our Common Good

"We do not invite each other simply to eat and drink, but to eat and drink together." —Plutarch

There's a small note pinned to my refrigerator asking me to bring ham biscuits to the church dinner. It's signed with a quick heart and a simple B. It's also two years old.

Although my husband and I both grew up in rural communities, neither of us grew up in the one where we now live, having moved here when Small Brick Church called him as pastor. We knew from the beginning that we wanted to live here long term. It was only an hour from his parents, and our children were beginning to need the kind of stability that comes from living with the same people for years rather than months. So we bought a house and started to put down roots.

But knowing that we wanted to live with this community is not the same thing as the community knowing whether they wanted to live with us. The established rhythms and distinct identity that we find so appealing of small communities also have a way of keeping outsiders at arm's length. Ours is the kind of community where children attend school in the same building their mothers, fathers, aunts, uncles, and even grandmothers and grandfathers once did.

It's the kind of community that believes that if something isn't broken, there's no need to fix it. The kind of community to guard who brings the ham biscuits to church dinners.

I have hope that our children will eventually be able to lay claim to being from here, but my husband and I will always be from Somewhere Else. To be fair, our great-granddaddies ruined our chances of being from here when they made the foolish decision to settle Somewhere Else in the first place. As it is, my husband and I lack the relational capital that comes from having enough cousins in the surrounding environs to guarantee immediate inclusion.

Despite not being connected to its past, we're doing our best to be part of its future by entering what Wendell Berry calls "the membership"—those people who recognize their shared responsibility to a place and take ownership for its well-being. Nathan's on the board of the Rec Club; I'm on the PTA. We take our turns at the Christmas tree lot and the annual Chicken BBQ and have helped organize community-wide worship services.

But it hasn't been without challenges. Even at church.

Besides being an outsider, I don't think I'm what folks had in mind for a pastor's wife. Sure, I can make pie and play the piano and wear my pearls. But I also grew up just far enough north to not know how to say "Yes, ma'am" and "No, ma'am" convincingly. I can be pretty stubborn when the moment calls for it. And my work as an author and speaker takes me away from home, if not on a frequent basis, at least a regular one.

So when Bea Cundiff handed me a slip of paper with the words "ham biscuits" on it, I knew something remarkable had happened.

Better Together

To be entrusted with making the ham biscuits for a church dinner felt like being asked to carry the Olympic torch. But to have Bea

Cundiff entrust me with them felt like being asked to light the flame. Bea has been planning church socials for years, and she might just be the most efficient, most reliable, most methodical woman I've ever met. If she says she's going to do something, you know she will. She won't back out or forget. She is prompt, orderly, and regulated. She's everything I am not. Which is exactly why we need each other.

Just as none of us can pull off a church dinner on our own, none of us can become discerning on our own either. In fact, in his book *How to Think*, Alan Jacobs notes that none of us can actually think for ourselves. Designed to live in community, human beings process information and come to decisions in "necessarily, thoroughly, and wonderfully social" ways.[1] This can be hard to admit, especially for those of us who like to imagine ourselves independent thinkers. We can see how *other* people are influenced. When they offer an opinion, we think to ourselves: *Well, of course, you think that. Just look where you get your news. Look at what church you go to. Look at your family background* . . . But when *we* have an opinion, somehow we believe we reached it independently, through nothing but sheer, unassailable logic.

The truth is that the leaders we follow, the communities we're part of, and the organizations we support all play a role in shaping the decisions we make. That's why Proverbs predicts that "the one who walks with the wise will become wise, but a companion of fools will suffer harm."[2] It's also why Paul calls us with this next phrase

> THE LEADERS we follow, the communities we're part of, and the organizations we support all play a role in shaping the decisions we make.

in Philippians 4 to "do what you have learned and received and heard from me, and seen in me." Moving from the theoretical to the practical, he offers his own life as an example of how to find goodness by living out the principles he's just taught.

Initially this may sound like arrogance or a power grab, especially for those who've been part of authoritarian religious communities. But remember that Paul's goal has always been to teach us *how* to think, not what to think. When Paul calls us to follow him, he knows that we will be following *someone*, so it's important that we follow someone who is following Christ.[3] He's also affirming the importance of seeking wisdom through community. Even if we *could* think for ourselves, we'd be foolish to do so. None of us are so wise, so educated, so experienced, or so insightful as to be able to see everything clearly all the time. "A fool's way is right in his own eyes," Proverbs 12:15 warns, "but whoever listens to counsel is wise."

The fact that discernment comes in and through community also means that we should be suspicious of people who refuse to submit themselves to the accountability of community or who posture themselves as having a corner on truth. If someone is teaching or saying something that no one else is, there's usually a reason for that. And it's rarely good. Instead of seeking a private experience of wisdom, we are seeking common wisdom. The road may be narrow, but we are not alone on it.

Potluck

One of my favorite things about church dinners is that they offer a window on my fellow church members, each person's dish representing a unique mix of personal taste, family tradition, and whatever is currently in their pantry. Even though we call it a potluck, some things are almost certain to be there: Bea will arrange for fried chicken, Jeanie will bring her tomato bake, and her sister Mag will bring her chocolate cake with the fudge icing that's as thick as the cake itself. I've also noticed that the dishes, like the layers of strata at an archaeological dig, reveal different culinary ages. Older folks seem to prefer vintage recipes like molded Jell-O, meatloaf, and pimento cheese on perfect white bread triangles. Sometimes they'll even bring them in pristine Pyrex and original Tupperware. Their daughters, meanwhile, prefer Pampered Chef and layered taco salads and fruit dips.

While our differences in age and family background make for a good church potluck, they can just as quickly become a source of frustration and division. What one person loves, another hates. What one person thinks is good, another cannot abide. What are we to do when Christians come to very different conclusions about whether something is good or not? How can we give room for each other to exercise individual discernment while maintaining unity?

The early church struggled with this exact question, ironically, in the context of church dinners. Unlike the members of our church who share the same sociological heritage, the believers in the early church came from many different cultural backgrounds. Some were rich, some poor. Some from the servant class, some wealthy elites. Some were Jews who confessed Jesus as Messiah; some were pagans who had once revered Diana and Apollo. All were believers and all worshiped the same Lord, but the differences in their pasts meant they had different convictions about which foods were good. Some ate only vegetables. Others would eat meat but only meat that aligned with Jewish dietary laws. (No ham biscuits.) Still others would eat nonkosher meats but not if it had previously been offered to idols in temple rituals. Some thought nothing of eating meat sold at the temple stalls.

Part of the problem for early Christians was that food was more than sustenance. Food was culture. Like today, food represents a larger set of experiences that make up who we are, and when the believers at Rome gathered together to eat, they brought all of this to the table. Very quickly, the cultural differences between them became a source of contention and judgment, an irritant that threatened to choke the life from the Body.

In many ways, what was happening to the church at Rome is similar to what happens when a person with food allergies tries to eat at a potluck. When he was three, my youngest son was diagnosed with tree nut allergies, which, thankfully, are not severe, but we still guard him, knowing that this could change at any time. It's fairly easy at home, but church dinners are another thing entirely. He's old enough to ask what's in a dish and avoid things that obviously have nuts. His brother and sister look out for him, and church folks keep an eye on him too. But it's always in the back of my mind: all it takes is one innocent cookie to trigger a reaction.

Allergic reactions happen when a person's immune system, which is responsible to identify and resist disease, becomes overactive and incorrectly identifies *good* things—eggs, dairy products, wheat, tree nuts—as threats. Allergies develop for many different reasons, including early exposure and family history, but once you have them, it doesn't really matter how you got them. Your focus turns to limiting your exposure and knowing how to stop a reaction once it starts. Depending on the individual, reactions can range from the relatively minor symptoms of watery eyes, runny nose, and itching to the more severe, even life-threatening, symptoms of anaphylaxis.

Like the human body, the Body of Christ has mechanisms to identify contaminating influences and expel them. But sometimes, the Body can become sensitized and mistake good things as threats and, in an effort to protect itself, will end up attacking itself. This is exactly what happened to the believers at Rome. Each member and faction had turned on the other, passing judgment for their choices, both to eat as well as to abstain from certain foods. In so doing, Paul says, they were destroying the work of God.

A Pound of Cure

The terrifying thing about a severe allergic reaction is that, technically, the allergen does not harm the body; the reaction does. So once a reaction begins, it's essential to stop it. To arrest the believers at Rome, Paul speaks pointedly to them, reminding them that only One person has the right to judge their choices about what is good: "Who are you to judge another's household servant?" he asks.

> Whoever eats, eats for the Lord, since he gives thanks to God;
> and whoever does not eat, it is for the Lord that he does not
> eat it, and he give thanks to God. . . . Why do you despise your
> brother or sister? For we will all stand before the judgment seat of
> God. For it is written,
>
> > As I live, says the Lord,
> > every knee shall bow to me,
> > and every tongue will give praise to God.[4]

By reminding them that God is Lord, Paul overrides their self-destructive responses. Surprisingly, he does not call them to simply love each other despite their differences; he calls them to recognize how their infighting is harming their own spiritual growth as well as the larger ministry of the church. He reminds them of what holds them together in the first place, underscoring the truth that we can only seek the *common good* when something larger than our individual preferences unites us. Then to prevent further reactions, Paul speaks from his own experience, teaching them how to manage their sensitivities.

First he notes that the inability to consume something or participate in a certain activity does not necessarily make it bad. "I know and am persuaded in the Lord Jesus that nothing is unclean in itself. Still, to someone who considers a thing to be unclean, to that one it is unclean" (Rom. 14:14). Because of our personal history or experience, we may come to the conviction that we can't engage in a certain activity—that this activity is not good *for us*—and so to pursue spiritual health and follow the Holy Spirit's leading, we avoid it.

But correspondingly, we must also understand that if we *are* able to consume something good, it doesn't mean that everyone else can too. Because of *their* personal history and experience, something may trigger a reaction for them that doesn't trigger a reaction in us. In order to pursue *their* spiritual health, it's essential that they avoid it as carefully as my son avoids nuts.[5] And because we love the Lord and we love them, we will walk sensitively with them through their sensitivities.[6]

We will alter our choices and practices to care for them. We will never "put a stumbling block or pitfall in the way of [our] brother or sister" (Rom. 14:13). We will make choices that protect him, never belittling, never mocking, never tempting him to partake of something that could endanger his life. "None of us lives for himself, and no one dies for himself," Paul reminds the believers. "Do not destroy, by what you eat, someone for whom Christ died. . . . Do not tear down God's work because of food."[7]

With time, some people's bodies come to tolerate what they once couldn't; a food that once triggered a response may not years later. But for others, allergies are a way of life, and the best we can do is find a way to thrive despite them. We can't change the world around us, and we can't change our reactions, so we give attention to learning our body and enjoying the good foods that we can eat. We become self-aware. Likewise, seeking goodness in community means giving attention, not to how others need to change but to how we need to change, to practicing the age-old wisdom of being "strict with ourselves and generous with everyone else."

When it comes to differences, the world thinks that the best way to overcome them is to live and let live, but Scripture tells us that the best way to overcome differences is to love and let love. To love God, regardless of whether we choose to eat or drink; to love our neighbor as ourselves, regardless of whether she chooses to eat or drink as well. So that "whether you eat or drink, or whatever you do, do everything for the glory of God. Give no offense to Jews or Greeks or the church of God . . . not seeking [your] own benefit, but the benefit of many, so that they may be saved."[8]

The Gift of Discernment

While the Scripture encourages us to give up our liberties for the good of each other, the goal is not conformity. We sacrifice for each other *because* we are in relationship with each other, not *in order* to stay in relationship with each other. This nuance is essential because it helps us discern the difference between healthy and unhealthy communities.

> WE SACRIFICE for each other *because* we are in relationship with each other, not *in order* to stay in relationship with each other.

Because as much as healthy communities can lead us to wisdom and goodness, unhealthy communities can actually hinder our developing discernment.

Another point that Jacobs makes in *How to Think* is how often we conform to community expectations and toe the party line, not because we are convinced it's right or good, but because speaking out against it would jeopardize our membership in the group. Sometimes this may mean accepting bad treatment for ourselves, as in abusive relationships, or enabling the abuse of others, all in order to stay in the group. Jacobs says that we can tell the difference between an unhealthy community and a healthy one by its attitude toward discernment. An unhealthy community "discourages, mocks, and ruthlessly excludes those who ask uncomfortable questions. . . . The genuine community is open to thinking and questioning, so long as those thoughts and questions come from people of goodwill."[9]

In fact, the dissenting voice is so important to finding goodness that God has equipped certain people with a particular gift for discernment. Paul identifies this gifting in 1 Corinthians 12 as the ability to "distinguish between spirits" (v. 10). As John explains it in chapter 4 of his first epistle, this is the ability to identify false teachers from true ones—to know who is speaking in the name of God and who isn't. While we are all called to practice discernment, certain people have extra insight and clarity, and they use it the same way a healthy immune system protects the body by identifying and combating illness. "Discernment," writes Henri Nouwen, "is not about judging other people's motives. It's about distinguishing good guidance from harmful messages, and the Holy Spirit from evil spirits. This essential sorting . . . is intended for our protection and not for our judgment."[10]

But what happens when a community can't receive dissenting opinions? At the very least, it won't benefit from those with the gift of discernment, and because of the pressure to conform, those with the gift might be tempted to remain silent about the danger they see. But in the silence, the community risks coming under the control of false, manipulative leaders while those who do have insight from God are ignored. Correspondingly, those with the gift of discernment might become so frustrated that they are tempted to use it to judge and divide the Body, rather than heal it.

I find myself regularly tempted by this. I can remember distinct times of being frustrated with people who couldn't see what was so obvious to me. *Why can't they understand what's happening? Why can't they see that she's manipulating them with her smiles and niceties? What will it take for them to recognize that he's teaching falsehood?*

At one point, Nathan, tired of my angst, turned to me and said: "Hannah, if you actually have the gift of discernment, then you can't expect other people to have it too. You can't expect them to be who God has made *you* to be."

Here's the hard truth: If you are entrusted with a certain gift, most of the people around you won't be similarly gifted. They won't be able to see as clearly because God has not equipped them to. But being gifted with discernment does not give you permission to be spiteful, arrogant, or judgmental toward them. It is your responsibility to help the community by raising uncomfortable questions and then waiting patiently while it struggles with them. And more than likely, you'll have to wait much longer than you want.

Perhaps you've gained clarity about a systemic sin or a cultural tendency that is harming the Body. Because you can see the difference between good and evil so clearly, you'll want to raise the alarm—which you must. But precisely because the sin has become so common, it will be hard for others to see it as quickly as you see it. Or maybe you can see how a system that was good fifty years ago isn't necessarily good today. But because it's been fifty years in the making, it will also take time for others to understand that it needs to change. In either case, you will have to remember that you are part of the Body, you are part of something bigger than yourself. You will have to remember that the clarity you enjoy is not for you alone. It is for the healing of the *Body* of Christ.

If your experience is anything like mine, you will quite possibly feel alone in this. Instead of relishing being the "prophetic" voice, you'll agonize over it. If you truly have the gift of discernment, you'll also know the weight of what you are about to say. But because you see good and evil more clearly, you'll also see more clearly what's at risk, and like Jeremiah, even if you try to keep quiet, you'll find the weight of God's message stronger still: "I say, 'I won't mention him, or speak any longer in his name.' But his message becomes a burning fire in my heart, shut up in my bones. I become tired of holding it in, and I cannot" (20:9).

I know there have been times when I have sinned by silence and other times I have spoken in arrogance. I also know there are times when I have frustrated people by simply being a dissenting voice. I know some would prefer I be the proverbial meek and quiet female tasked with maintaining social norms. And if I'm honest, I'd prefer that too. As I've confessed to Nathan on more than one occasion, "I'd be anybody else if I could." But at the end of the day, none of us can tell God that He made a mistake in forming and gifting us in the way He has.[11] None of us can call unclean what He has called clean. None of us can call bad what He has called good.

And of all people, those with the gift of discernment should be the first to recognize that.

Discerning the Body

In the medieval world, Italian peasants used the idiomatic expression *vivere a uno pane e a uno vino* to describe belonging to the same family: "To live on one bread and one wine."[12] When Christ wanted to teach us the goodness of finding life together in Him,

He used the same imagery. On the very night that His closest friends would betray Him,

> the Lord Jesus took bread, and when he had given thanks, broke it, and said, "This is my body which is for you. . . ."
>
> In the same way also he took the cup, after supper, and said, "This cup is the new covenant in my blood. . . ." For as often as you eat this bread and drink the cup, you proclaim the Lord's death until he comes.[13]

Here is one bread and one wine and one body and one Lord and one life.

When we come to eat together at the table, we are seeking more than sustenance; we are seeking the goodness of belonging. Of belonging to Him and to each other. We are seeking the goodness of knowing we have a place, of knowing that there will always be room for us. We are seeking the goodness of home and family and community.

We are seeking something that many of us doubt is possible.

I don't think we're so naïve as to expect to find such welcome in the world around us. We know the brokenness that exists there; we've lived it in our families and schools and workplaces. But when it comes to the church, we long for something different. We long for a communion of goodness where we could—if only for a moment—be safe and secure. We long for the belonging that is promised in the bread and wine. But even here, the brokenness creeps. Even here, we must still discern between good and evil. Even here, we experience pain, confusion, loss, and rejection. And so as we learn to not retreat from the world, we find ourselves retreating from the church. We find ourselves guarded and withdrawn. We find ourselves unable to see the goodness that still exists there.

But I wonder if this isn't exactly the point of the Lord's table, the table that belongs to the One who broke bread in the presence of His enemies, whose cup overflowed as He dipped the morsel and gave it to the very friend who would betray Him. The table that even today welcomes those who will crush Him, who will break His body with their teeth and consume His blood and take His life to sustain their own.[14]

> IN COMING to the table, we are forced to reckon with the fact that nothing else is good enough to draw us together.

I wonder, as well, if part of testifying to the Lord's death *must* involve joining with those who have sinned against us and who we have sinned against. Because in coming to the table, we are forced to reckon with the fact that nothing else is good enough to draw us together. In coming together, we defy the brokenness and proclaim a greater, shared good. And I wonder if the Lord's broken body doesn't in some way mirror the brokenness of the body that limps and stumbles bleeding to the altar. As much as we must learn to discern goodness in the world around us, we must learn to discern it within His Body to see its goodness despite its brokenness. To know as Paul writes in 1 Corinthians 10:17 that "because there is one bread, we who are many are one body, since all of us share the one bread." To know the goodness of those with whom we "live on one bread and one wine."

This is no small thing, especially for those of us who have been harmed in churches, who have been betrayed, devalued, and manipulated by those we thought we could trust. Such wounds do not heal easily, and when they do, they scar. *But who better to understand this than the One who carries the scars of betrayal in His own body? Who better to understand this than the One who offers us His broken, bleeding self for our healing and resurrection?* So that as we come to the table, we can't help but remember that He was broken long before we were. We can't help but remember His willing sacrifice. We can't help but remember that the God who led Him through the valley of the shadow of death and raised Him to new life will one day prepare a table for those who come from east and west and from every tribe and tongue and nation to partake of His goodness.

Surely, this God can cause goodness and mercy to follow us, too. Surely this God can make a way for us to dwell in His house forever.

The Goodness of the Lord

Every church has its struggles. Tucked away, down a road that meanders past fields and barns, up hills and around bends, ours is no exception. This year we will be ninety-six years old, and we feel every bit of it. But every fall, we gather to celebrate our years on this beautiful, broken earth. We call it "Homecoming" because that's what it feels like—a family reunion where friends and former members come back to visit. For days before, we'll bake and cook and plan and prep. We'll bring in a special preacher, and Wade will bring out his guitar. If we're lucky, the grannies will sing "It's Not an Easy Road" in three-part harmony, and Randy will come up from Georgia to play his harmonica. We will testify and pray and tell stories from the past: how we originally met in a tent, how Anita's daddy helped dig out the sanctuary basement and Carol's granddaddy built the walls, how the bell used to echo through the surrounding hills. There are stories of darker times too. Of conflict, selfishness, division. Of loss and pain. We can see who is missing—who should be there but isn't. But we don't like to talk about that much. We'll go quiet and gaze off for a moment as we wonder whether things could have turned out differently. And we'll wish they had.

But once what needs to be said is said and what needs to be sung is sung, we'll head down to a pavilion on the edge of the woods where a quiet stream trickles past. And there, like a table in the wilderness, goodness will be waiting for us in the form of fried chicken, hash brown casserole, ham biscuits, deviled eggs, and Crock-Pot upon Crock-Pot of baked beans. A second table will hold salads: twenty-four hour, three-bean, fruit, and Jell-O—the pistachio with maraschino cherries on the top and the strawberry with pretzels on the bottom. We'll load our plates while we eye the banana pudding, berry cobbler, and Mag's chocolate cake with fudge icing as thick as the cake itself.

And then under the sycamores and maples and oaks, on hard wooden benches and even harder metal folding chairs, we will gather together, and we will feast on all that's good.

Benediction
(for further study)

"God saw all that he had made, and it was very good indeed." —Gen. 1:31

The word "benediction" comes from two Latin roots which, when taken together, literally mean "a good word." More colloquially, we know a benediction as the final blessing at the close of a worship service. But this "good word" isn't simply an end to a time of reflection and learning; it's also a beginning, the bridge back to the world of being and doing. Perhaps that's why the Scripture *opens* with God blessing the world that He has made. More than simply ending His creative work, this benediction propels us out into it with confidence and hope.

But you know as well as I do that the Scripture also speaks of the brokenness of the world. Yes, the world is full of goodness, but here, in the spaces that we inhabit, that goodness is often hidden, obscured by our selfishness and sin. So difficult is it to see goodness that Jesus tells us that we must search for it. Precisely because it's not always apparent, we must *seek* the kingdom of heaven. But when we seek, we're confident we will find; when we ask, we're confident He will answer. We're confident that even as we work out our salvation with fear and trembling, He's already working in us both to will and to work according to His good purposes.

We're confident that the God who once made all things good will make all things good once again.

And it's this confidence—not in the goodness of the world itself but in the goodness of God—that allows us to move forward, to leave these moments of wonder and worship and commit ourselves to the work of learning discernment. These final pages are designed to help you in that process. They include a brief review of the principles of each chapter, questions for reflection, further reading, and a proverb to memorize—all in an effort to move these things from your head through your heart to your hands. And because discernment is learned best in community, please consider doing this work with friends, family, or fellow church members. Gather around a table, meet in a living room, or assemble in a classroom; and as you do, experience the goodness of being made good together.

> Finally brothers and sisters, whatever is true, whatever is honorable, whatever is just, whatever is pure, whatever is lovely, whatever is commendable—if there is any moral excellence and if there is anything praiseworthy—dwell on these things. Do what you have learned and received and heard from me, and seen in me, and the God of peace will be with you. (Phil. 4:8–9)

CHAPTER 1—TASTE AND SEE

Review:

- Wise people are humble people who know that they need wisdom. A person whose life is defined by pride or arrogance is not a trustworthy guide to goodness.
- Discernment means knowing the difference between good and bad; knowing a lot of information or making the "right" choices does not guarantee that a person is discerning.
- Only people who are willing to change and grow will find goodness; people looking for quick solutions to complicated problems will not become wise.

Reflect:

1. What most unsettles or concerns you about the world we live in? Do you find your concern has increased or decreased as you have grown older? If it has, what has changed?

2. Do you consider yourself a discerning person? Why or why not? Name a person you know in real life who you consider to be a wise, discerning person, and then describe them.

3. Remember a time you were tricked by someone or you made a foolish choice. What do you think contributed to the situation? How did you feel once you realized what had happened?

4. Proverbs teaches that humility ("the fear of the Lord") is the first step to cultivating discernment. What does this imply about people who display traits of pride or arrogance? How does pride short-circuit our decisions?

5. What do you think of the statement "The goal of discernment . . . is to learn what is good so that we might embrace and enjoy it"? How does it differ from what you've heard about discernment in the past?

Read: 1 Kings 3:3–15

Remember: "The fear of the LORD is the beginning of knowledge; fools despise wisdom and instruction." Proverbs 1:7 (ESV)

CHAPTER 2—THE GOOD EARTH

Review:

- In order to find goodness, we must be willing to leave our comfort zones and safe spaces to engage the world God has made.
- Discernment looks past superficial conditions to see the true nature of something.
- Because discernment sees both the good and bad, it is neither idealistic nor pessimistic. It affirms the brokenness of the world as well as God's ongoing work of redemption.

Reflect:

1. When you look at the world around you, do you see it positively or negatively? What things or experiences might affect how a person sees the world and whether they believe goodness exists in it?

2. Chapter 2 explores the idea of information comfort zones or "filter bubbles." What institutions or people do you turn to for information? Why do you trust them? What is the difference between a trusted source of information and a filter bubble?

3. What habits, traditions, or practices bring you comfort in the chaos of the world? How might these things be a reminder of God's goodness? How might they hinder discernment?

4. Given the brokenness of the world, does it surprise you that Scripture speaks about its goodness? How does discernment

make us both realistic and hopeful about the condition of the world and our own lives?

5. How does it change your understanding of discernment to think of it in terms of redemption and spiritual transformation rather than retreat from the world? Which demands more of you?

Read: Romans 8:18–30

Remember: "The LORD founded the earth by wisdom and established the heavens by understanding." Proverbs 3:19

CHAPTER 3—WORLDLY WISE

Review:

- Discerning people know the difference between lasting goodness and temporary pleasure and seek things that satisfy both body and soul.
- God's good gifts are intended to draw us back to Him in gratitude and humility. We must neither reject the gift nor love it more than the Giver.
- Discernment is a process of spiritual transformation. Instead of taking us out of the world, God is making us holy in it, teaching us how to love and pursue goodness that lasts.

Reflect:

1. How have you heard "worldliness" defined in the past? How did you understand it before reading this chapter? Has your perception of what is "worldly" changed?

2. Think of something that God has given you that has led you to experience His goodness in a deeper, richer way. How could

that same thing end up distracting you from Him? What keeps a blessing from becoming a stumbling block?

3. When Jesus tells us to "store up treasure in heaven," He's making a point about the kinds of things that our hearts should long for, not simply whether something is "spiritual." Share something mundane that you do every day that has eternal value.

4. Do you generally trust religious organizations, or are you suspicious of them? Why is discernment necessary even (especially) in religious communities?

5. Part of learning discernment means training our hearts to love good things. As you consider the course of your spiritual life, can you see growth or change in what your heart loves? What things were once difficult for you to love that you now find easy?

Read: Proverbs 8:1–21

Remember: "Wisdom is supreme—so get wisdom. And whatever else you get, get understanding." Proverbs 4:7

CHAPTER 4—WHATEVER IS TRUE

Review:

- Shared truth is essential to flourishing community. Falsehood and private interpretations of facts lead to division and fractured relationships.

- Wise people handle facts with integrity and are willing to question their own motives and emotions.

- Emotions can tell us that something is wrong, but they can't tell us what is wrong or who is responsible. In themselves, emotions also cannot confirm that something is right or good.

Reflect:

1. In what specific ways do you see truth under assault in broader culture? How has it come under assault in the church? What does this make you think and feel?

2. In your own words, describe a person who seeks truth and is truthful. How do they handle information? How do they speak? How do they handle conflict? Would you consider yourself a truthful person?

3. How can our emotions or feelings of loyalty hinder the search for truth? What's at risk if we don't identify the role these things play in our decision making?

4. Can you think of a time when someone presented a truthful thing in an untruthful way? Perhaps a verse of Scripture taken out of context or facts manipulated to promote a certain ideology? How long did it take you to realize that they were mishandling truth? How did you know?

5. Why do you think it is so hard for us to seek truth? How does the gospel free us to pursue truth without fear?

Read: 2 Peter 1:16–21

Remember: "A truthful witness rescues lives, but one who utters lies is deceitful." Proverbs 14:25

CHAPTER 5—WHATEVER IS HONORABLE

Review:

- We must seek our value from God, not from what other people think of us. This frees us to make decisions that are truly good rather than pleasing other people.

- Wise people honor the wisdom of others, humbly receiving advice and instruction from those with more experience, skill, or knowledge in a certain area.
- In order to glorify Himself, God honors unexpected things, including things and people that society deems worthless. We cannot trust society to tell us what is worth honoring.

Reflect:

1. Have you or someone you know ever discovered something valuable in the trash or at a thrift store or flea market? What does this teach us about our understanding of honor?

2. Do you find yourself seeking honor from other people, making choices or crafting a certain image to gain their favor? How does this hinder discernment? How does knowing that God crowns His image bearers with honor free us to make good decisions?

3. As society becomes polarized, we'll be tempted to dishonor those with whom we disagree. Do you feel unfairly judged or dishonored because of your opinions? How have you unfairly judged or dishonored people with opposing opinions?

4. Remember a time when you felt intimidated or uncomfortable by someone's expertise. What do you think prompted your discomfort? Was it personal insecurity? Their elitism? A bit of both?

5. The Scripture teaches that God often honors unexpected things. What specific people or things does God honor that our society does not? How can we know what is worthy of honor?

Read: 1 Corinthians 1:26–2:5

Remember: "A mocker doesn't love one who corrects him; he will not consult the wise." Proverbs 15:12

Chapter 6—Whatever Is Just

Review:

- Human beings have an innate sense of fairness, but our sense that something is not right is not enough to explain what is wrong.
- We discover what is just ("the ways things are supposed to be") by natural revelation, the Scripture, and the person of Jesus Christ.
- Grace frees us from using rules and regulations for self-justification. Because we have already been justified though Christ, we can risk having our own injustice corrected, even as we seek justice more broadly.

Reflect:

1. What situations or events stir your sense of justice? What things make you want to scream, "That's not fair!"? What other feelings can accompany a sense of injustice?
2. Does the holistic relationship between natural revelation, Scripture, and the person of Jesus Christ surprise you? What does this mean for how we interpret Scripture and how we understand Jesus' teaching?
3. Can you think of anything that feels "natural" to you that is challenged or adjusted by Scripture? How does something like grace or mercy disrupt our natural sense of justice?
4. It's possible to be an expert in the rules and still be unwise. How would you recognize if someone is using the Scripture to justify themselves instead of seeking goodness? How would you recognize if you are using it that way?

5. How does God's forgiving our sin and justifying us by faith free us to seek justice in the world? What does it allow us to do when confronted with our own injustice?

Read: Romans 3:21–31

Remember: "Doing what is righteous and just is more acceptable to the LORD than sacrifice." Proverbs 21:3

CHAPTER 7—WHATEVER IS PURE

Review:

- The choices we make in our private lives predict the choices we will make in our public lives, and how we use our bodies reveals the state of our hearts.
- Being naïve is not the same as being discerning and can put us at risk for manipulation. Discerning people can identify what both good and evil look like.
- God makes us wise by purifying us of our mixed motives and healing our fractured hearts. Only then can we truly seek what is good and be innocent of evil.

Reflect:

1. Polls suggest that both Christians and broader society increasingly do not see a link between private morality and public service. What do you think? Do our private choices interact with our public roles and responsibilities? If so, how? If not, why not?
2. Consider the statement, "Adultery did not make [the priests] impure; they committed adultery because they were already impure. They had divided hearts. . . . The choices we make

sexually reveal our heart's posture toward God and each other." Do you agree or disagree with this framing? How does this framing change your understanding of sexual sin?

3. Some folks accuse Christians of being obsessed with sex—that we spend more time talking about sexual ethics than other sins. Do you think this is a valid complaint? What do we get right in our conversations about sex? What do we get wrong?

4. In your own words, explain the difference between sexual naïveté and sexual purity. Why is naïveté insufficient preparation for knowing the difference between what's good and what's bad?

5. Does the thought of Christ's coming as a refiner's fire scare you or excite you? Does it feel like a threat or a promise?

Read: Malachi 3:13–4:4

Remember: "A crucible for silver, and a smelter for gold, and the Lord is the tester of hearts." Proverbs 17:3

Chapter 8—Whatever Is Lovely

Review:

- Beauty leads us to goodness by turning earthly value systems on their heads and pointing us to greater realities. Sometimes good things will not make economic sense on this earth.

- Our hearts often love good things in wrong ways. Instead of simply rejecting lovely things, God wants us to learn to love them the way He loves them.

- Good people protect the loveliness of other people, honoring them as image bearers instead of trying to possess their beauty for themselves.

Reflect:

1. Try to remember a time when you chose something beautiful over something practical. Or a time when you wanted to choose something beautiful but didn't. Why did you choose one over the other?

2. What's your initial reaction to the idea that Christ found you lovely enough to sacrifice for? What does this say about Him? What does it say about you? How does it make you feel about Him in response?

3. What are some differences between how secular society pursues and understands beauty and how Christians should pursue and understand beauty? What is the goal of beauty for secular society? What is the goal for Christians?

4. Do you think it is possible for men and women to recognize each other's loveliness without succumbing to lust or sexual impropriety? What stands in the way of this kind of relationship?

5. In John 12:32, Jesus says, "If I am lifted up from the earth I will draw all people to myself." What do you find most beautiful and compelling about Christ—what draws you to Him?

Read: Matthew 19:16–30

Remember: "For wisdom is better than jewels, and nothing desirable can equal it." Proverbs 8:11

Chapter 9—Whatever Is Commendable

Review:

- Wise people know the power of their words. What we choose to speak about and how we choose to speak about it can either build up or destroy.

- Our words reveal the state of our hearts, whether we are storing up goodness or evil in them. We will give account for the words we say because they reflect this greater reality.
- Discerning people speak appropriately about both good and bad; instead of being silent, they will use their words to praise what is good and condemn what is evil.

Reflect:

1. Think of a time when you regretted saying something or when you regretted *not* saying something. What other emotions did you feel in that moment? Why do you regret your choice?
2. In the digital age, opinions are commonplace and words abundant. How does such a large supply of words affect their value? Do you believe that *your* words are powerful and have value? Why or why not?
3. In some ways, speech is freer, livelier, and more powerful than it's ever been. What responsibility do we have for what we say online or in public spaces? What is the difference between regulating people's freedom of speech and holding each other accountable to "speak well"?
4. Seeking whatever is commendable means speaking positively about good things and negatively about evil things. Which do you find more difficult? Do you find it easy to be overly critical of good things? Or do you find yourself uncritically affirming everything?
5. Most people do not have public platforms, a mass following, or leadership positions, but we do have our own private spheres of influence. How are you stewarding your voice in the space where God has placed you?

Read: Ephesians 5:1–20

Remember: "The tongue that heals is a tree of life, but a devious tongue breaks the spirit." Proverbs 15:4

Chapter 10—Every Good Gift

Review:

- We live in the "already, not yet"—waiting for full redemption. We must make choices with an eye to both our present brokenness and Christ's return.
- Developing virtue gives us the skills we need to make good decisions regardless of what life throws at us.
- Everything, even something good, has a cost. Discernment means knowing the difference between what is good and what is better, between what is permissible and what is beneficial.

Reflect:

1. Do you like thrift stores? Why or why not? Do you think thrifting is an appropriate metaphor for discerning goodness in the world? Why or why not?

2. In many ways, rules are easier to follow than principles because rules are explicit. Which do you think is a more effective approach to making good decisions? Why? In what ways is virtue-based decision-making harder than rule-based decision-making?

3 Is your initial response to the word "pragmatic" positive or negative? How have you seen pragmatism abused? Why is "principled pragmatism" necessary for discernment?

4. How often do you find yourself paralyzed by the fear of making a bad decision? What do you think contributes to your fear?

Why might making a mistake feel more dangerous than not making a decision at all?

5. Even good things come at a cost. Do you find it difficult to walk away from good things? If so, why do you think it is hard for you to give up good things?

Read: Matthew 13:24–43

Remember: "If you seek it like silver and search for it like hidden treasure, then you will understand the fear of the LORD and discover the knowledge of God." Proverbs 2:4–5

CHAPTER 11—OUR COMMON GOOD

Review:

• We cannot "think for ourselves." Because humans are relational, our thinking and decision-making is affected by the company we keep.

• Our personal histories influence decision-making, leading good people to have different views on what is "good" and "bad." When preferences conflict, wise people are strict with themselves and generous with others.

• Unity for the sake of unity is not good or discerning. Sometimes seeking goodness will mean voicing an unpopular opinion for the health and healing of the community.

Reflect:

1. How can community be an asset to discernment? How can it hinder it? How would you know whether a community is supporting or hindering the development of discernment?

2. Give some examples of preferences that divide Christian community. Have your views on any of these things shifted over the years? What do you think contributed to that shift?

3. What is the difference between the advice to "live and let live" and the Christian call to unity? What ultimately holds Christian community together?

4. Have you ever been called to be a dissenting voice within your community? What temptations did you face in speaking up?

5. How has the church been a place of goodness for you? How has it been a place of suffering? How does discernment help you make peace with this tension?

Read: Romans 14:1–15:6

Remember: "The one who walks with the wise will become wise, but a companion of fools will suffer harm." Proverbs 13:20

Acknowledgments

Gratitude is nothing more than taking time to acknowledge the good things in your life, pausing long enough to see the goodness around you. I suppose in some sense, then, gratitude is a natural part of discernment, and I'd be foolish to overlook the good people who have made this book possible.

Nathan, what a life we have found together! Who knew it would be filled with such beauty and goodness?

Phoebe, Harry, and Peter, I can't wait to see all the good things God has in store for you.

Friends and family, far and near—may we truly be God's gifts to each other.

Heather, for more than you'll ever know.

Kim, your faith and resilience testify to His goodness.

"The Second Best Family," for walking through life with ours.

Erin, our chats are a constant source of encouragement and blessing.

Erik W., agent in this work of writing.

The team at Moody, especially Judy, Ashley, Amanda, and Erik P. —let's do it all again soon!

And finally, the members of Christ and Pop Culture whose friendship, prayers, and conversation have challenged me to look for (and find!) all that is true, honorable, pure, just, lovely, and commendable in this life . . . and the next.

Notes

Chapter 1: Taste and See

1. Daniel J. Levitin, introduction to *The Organized Mind: Thinking Straight in the Age of Information Overload* (New York: Dutton, 2016), xx.
2. 1 Kings 3:7–9.
3. Proverbs 1:2–4 (ESV).
4. Proverbs 2:9–12, 20.

Chapter 2: The Good Earth

1. Eli Pariser, "Invisible Sieve: The Dangers of the Internet," *The Economist* (US), July 2, 2011, 71.
2. Charlotte Higgins, "The Hygge Conspiracy," *The Guardian*, November 22, 2016, https://www.theguardian.com/lifeandstyle/2016/nov/22/hygge-conspiracy-denmark-cosiness-trend.
3. This quote can be found in the collection of philosophy and theology observations published after Pascal's death in 1662, titled simply *Pensées*, or *Thoughts*.
4. Meik Wiking, *The Little Book of Hygge: Danish Secrets to Happy Living* (Waterville, ME: Thorndike Press, a Part of Gale, Cengage Learning, 2017), 47.
5. It seems that even a mother goddess cannot use the bathroom alone.
6. Maxwell Lincoln Anderson, *The Quality Instinct: Seeing Art through a Museum Director's Eye* (Washington, D.C.: AAM Press, American Association of Museums, 2013), 29–30.
7. Psalm 33:5 (KJV).
8. Genesis 1:28; 2:16.
9. C. S. Lewis, *Mere Christianity*, a revised and amplified edition, with a new introduction of the three books *Broadcast Talks, Christian Behaviour,* and *Beyond Personality* (New York: HarperOne, 2001), 38.
10. Henri J. M. Nouwen, Rebecca Laird, and Michael J. Christensen, *Discernment: Reading the Signs of Daily Life* (New York: HarperOne, 2015), 6.
11. Romans 12:2.

Chapter 3: Worldly Wise

1. Carl Philipp Emanuel Bach (1714–1788) was the son of Johann Sebastian Bach.

2. I do wonder whether our struggle to maintain funding for the arts is linked to the broader secularization of society, the church having long been a patron of musicians and visual and dramatic artists. Plus, what happens to the arts when we don't believe in the Transcendent anymore?

3. Ecclesiastes 2:1, 10.

4. Ecclesiastes 2:11.

5. Matthew 6:19–21.

6. 1 John 2:15–17: "Do not love the world or the things in the world. . . . the world is passing away along with its desires, but whoever does the will of God abides forever" (ESV).

7. Giles Slade, *Made to Break: Technology and Obsolescence in America* (Cambridge, MA: Harvard University Press, 2007), 50.

8. Part of the larger fallout of consumerism is that we can adopt a "throwaway ethic"—a lifestyle that disposes of something once it stops serving our needs or no longer makes us happy. But while it's one thing to throw away a disposable razor, it's another thing entirely to throw away a marriage.

9. Ecclesiastes 2:25–26 (ESV).

10. Ecclesiastes 3:1, 12–13 (ESV).

11. When Pete Seeger conceptualized this portion of Scripture as a folk ballad in the late 1950s, he introduced the phrase "turn, turn, turn," underscoring the cyclical nature of our lives.

12. James 1:16–17.

13. Luke 11:38–42.

14. Luke 14:5.

15. John 17:15–18.

16. James K. A. Smith, *Desiring the Kingdom: Worship, Worldview, and Cultural Formation* (Grand Rapids, MI: Baker Academic, 2011), 69.

17. Elaine Scarry, *On Beauty and Being Just* (Princeton, NJ: Princeton University Press, 1999), 87.

18. The larger framing of Proverbs affirms the connection between virtue and discernment, as it seems more concerned with making wise people than wise decisions. The goal of wisdom literature is to change who we are at a fundamental level.

Chapter 4: Whatever Is True

1. I'm not the only one to find a role model in Nancy Drew. In a 2009 article, Mary Jo Murphy traces her influence on three female members of the United States Supreme Court: Sandra Day O'Connor, Ruth Bader Ginsberg, and Sonia Sotomayor. Mary Jo Murphy, "Nancy Drew and the Secret of the 3 Black Robes," *The New York Times*, May 30, 2009, https://www.nytimes.com/2009/05/31/weekinreview/31murphy.html.

2. Wilson underestimated the public's love of detective stories and was flooded with angry mail trying to convince him that his dislike of them was unfounded. He wrote a follow-up piece in 1945, "Who Cares Who Killed Roger Ackroyd?" doubling down on his previous sentiment.

3. Edmund Wilson, "Why Do People Read Detective Stories?," *The New Yorker*, June 19, 2017, https://www.newyorker.com/magazine/1944/10/14/why-do-people-read-detective-stories.

4. Kurt Andersen, "How America Lost Its Mind," *The Atlantic*, September 2017, 78–91.

5. Jennifer Jackson, "The Detection Club: 10 Rules for Writing a Mystery," *Murder & Mayhem*, August 29, 2017, https://murder-mayhem.com/the-detection-club-rules.

6. Both the Old and New Testaments call us to test the credibility of prophets.

7. T. S. Eliot, "The Perfect Critic," in *The Sacred Wood: Essays on Poetry and Criticism* (1920): 9–10, quoted in Alan Jacobs, *How to Think* (New York: Currency, 2017), 22.

8. Early, sensationalized mystery novels were notorious for their racist undertones. When we feel a need for resolution for social problems, we often blame innocent people, with outliers and foreigners being the easiest target.

9. Psalm 51:6 (KJV).

10. "6 September (1955): Flannery O'Connor to Betsey Hester" (letter), *The American Reader* online.

11. Matthew 6:24.

12. James 1:8.

13. Ephesians 1:18 (KJV).

14. John 16:13.

15. In John 17:17, Jesus prays, "Sanctify them by the truth; your word is truth."

16. Mark A. Noll, *The Scandal of the Evangelical Mind* (Grand Rapids, MI: Eerdmans, 1994), 14.

17. Sometimes people reject uncomfortable information by claiming that "you can make facts say whatever you want." We cannot make facts say what we want, but we can say what we want about facts and frame them in a way that misconstrues them.

18. Knowing the power of truth, it is not surprising that some of the most gifted and prolific members of the Detection Club advocated for the power of shared truth within public spaces. Writers like G. K. Chesterton and Dorothy L. Sayers carried their passion for truth into their non-fiction work, arguing effectively and beautifully for its power and necessity.

19. Proverbs 3:3 (ESV).

Chapter 5: Whatever Is Honorable

1. "Carl Raymond Blair," Obituary, Greenville, SC, Dignity Memorial, accessed March 24, 2018, https://www.dignitymemorial.com/obituaries/greenville-sc/carl-blair-7734557.

2. Blair himself did not realize he was color blind until college when he completed a self-portrait in green, which prompted his teacher, a Professor Green, to believe he was mocking him. He was not. (Stephanie Trotter, "Modern Man," *TOWN*, accessed March 24, 2018, https://towncarolina.com/article/modern-man/.)

3. 1 Timothy 3:8, 11; Titus 2:2.

4. 2 Corinthians 4:17.

5. Susan Harding, "Representing Fundamentalism: The Problem of the Repugnant Cultural Other," *Social Research* 58, no. 2 (1991): 373–93, http://www.jstor.org/stable/40970650.

6. Brené Brown, *Braving the Wilderness: The Quest for True Belonging and the Courage to Stand Alone* (Waterville, ME: Thorndike Press, 2018), 75–76.

7. James 3:9.

8. 1 Peter 2:13–3:2.

9. Tom Nichols, *The Death of Expertise: The Campaign against Established Knowledge and Why It Matters* (New York: Oxford University Press, 2017), 15.

10. In times of persecution, the role of elder takes on more significance than it may in times of peace. As the public face of the church, the elders would be first targeted for imprisonment and martyrdom.

11. 1 Corinthians 1:19.

12. 1 Corinthians 1:26–27.

13. While we must be careful not to impose categorical characteristics on individual people, sociological data suggests that women and men *as classes* differ profoundly, not in their overall strength, but in their motivations and logic for why and how they go about doing things.

14. The previous logic applies not only to gender but equally to any person, group, or identity that established society does not honor as valuable, including children, the poor, the elderly, the disabled, and cultural and ethnic minorities.

15. 1 Corinthians 1:29.

16. Revelation 5:13.

Chapter 6: Whatever Is Just

1. Eurogame enthusiasts credit the 1995 game *Settlers of Catan* with sparking a new wave of board games characterized by innovation in play, artwork, and strategy and resulting in a $10-billion-a-year industry.

2. Bethany H. Hoang and Kristen D. Johnson, *The Justice Calling: Where Passion Meets Perseverance* (Grand Rapids, MI: Brazos Press, 2016), 10–11.

3. 1 Peter 1:16, quoting Leviticus 11:44–45; 19:2; 20:7.

4. Historians often note similarity between the Ten Commandments and other ancient legal codes, but rather than diminishing the significance of the Ten Commandments, the similarity reinforces the argument that these laws derive from something other than human culture or experience.

5. C. S. Lewis, *The Abolition of Man* (San Francisco: HarperCollins, 2001), 43.

6. Romans 2:14–15.

7. Surprisingly, while that particular game included a scientist, researcher, medic, dispatcher, and operations expert, it did not include an international legal expert.

8. In Titus 3:9–11, Paul warns the believers to avoid quarrels and controversies and to reject people who stir up division, calling them "warped and sinful" (esv).

9. Exodus 20 records that when Moses delivered the Ten Commandments to Israel, the people were afraid because they saw them as a source of judgment. Moses assures them the Law has been given, not to condemn them, but to *prevent* them from sinning, to teach them how to play the game the right way.

10. In Matthew 5:17–20, Jesus explains his relationship to the Law and Prophets, affirming the importance of both.

11. Luke 4:18–19.

12. I recognize that this illustration is limited; my main point is that discerning what is good is a holistic process that must account for both general and specific revelation as well as the revelation of Christ Himself.

13. Seventeenth-century Scottish philosopher David Hume identified this as the "is—ought problem," and so sometimes it is known as Hume's Law.

We may be able to describe the way something is, but this does not mean it should be that way.

14. First Corinthians 7:17–24 is a fascinating case study on the dynamic between God's providence in our lives and the choices we make within that providence.

15. Romans 3:25–26 (ESV).

16. Timothy Keller, *Generous Justice: How God's Grace Makes Us Just* (New York: Penguin Books, 2010), 40.

Chapter 7: Whatever Is Pure

1. Popularized by the late evangelist, the Billy Graham Rule is a private code of conduct in which a man commits to never dine, travel, or meet alone with a woman who is not his wife. Though the rule is followed primarily by men, some women also follow this practice in their interactions with men.

2. "Backing Trump, White Evangelicals Flip Flop on Importance of Candidate Character | PRRI/Brookings Survey," PRRI, October 19, 2016, https://www.prri.org/research/prri-brookings-oct-19-poll-politics-election-clinton-double-digit-lead-trump/.

3. The full account is found in Malachi 2:1–3:4.

4. Interestingly, the English word purity comes from the Greek root for fire (*pyr*) because in the ancient world, fire produced the heat necessary to remove impurities from metal. In Philippians 4:8, Paul actually uses the synonym *hagnos*, which conveys the same idea of being whole or uncontaminated.

5. Paul teaches the same principle in Titus 1:15: "To the pure, all things are pure, but to the defiled and unbelieving, nothing is pure; but both their minds and their consciences are defiled. They profess to know God, but they deny him by their works" (ESV).

6. The New Testament includes sexual integrity among the qualifications for church leaders based on the logic that behavior in the home predicts behavior in the church. See 1 Timothy 3:1–13.

7. When we justify impurity, the world becomes a dangerous, violent place, especially for women and children, who rely on the structure of marriage for social stability. In addressing the priest's infidelity, the Lord likens it to brutality: "For the man who does not love his wife but divorces her, says the Lord, the God Israel, covers his garment with violence" (Mal. 2:16 ESV).

8. Proverbs 22:3.

9. Proverbs 1:4.

10. Proverbs 7:21–23. The fact that Solomon uses the illustration of a young man does not imply that all women are inherently seductive. As often as Solomon warns young men against foolish women, he also compels them to seek out wise women (even presenting wisdom as feminine), promising that they will find security with women of virtue.

11. Tweet via @Alyssa_Milano, October, 15, 2017, https://twitter.com/alyssa_milano/status/919665538393083904.

12. Christen A. Johnson, "#MeToo: A Timeline of Events," Chicagotribune.com, March 19, 2018, http://www.chicagotribune.com/lifestyles/ct-me-too-timeline-20171208-htmlstory.html.

13. "What Teenagers Are Learning from Online Porn," *The New York Times*, February 12, 2018, https://mobile.nytimes.com/2018/02/07/magazine/teenagers-learning-online-porn-literacy-sex-education.html?referer=.

14. Emily F. Rothman, Courtney Kaczmarsky, Nina Burke, Emily Jansen and Allyson Baughman, "'Without Porn … I Wouldn't Know Half the Things I Know Now': A Qualitative Study of Pornography Use Among a Sample of Urban, Low-Income, Black and Hispanic Youth," *The Journal of Sex Research* 52, no. 7 (2014): 736–46.

15. Romans 16:17–18.

16. Proverbs 20:9.

17. 1 John 3:2. But who can see God and live? Or as Malachi 3:2 asks, "Who can endure the day of his coming? And who will be able to stand when he appears?" None of us. None of us can withstand the blaze of His glory. And that's precisely the point.

18. While the authorship of "How Firm a Foundation" is uncertain, this hymn was first published in 1787 by John Rippon in *A Selection of Hymns from the Best Authors, Intended to be an Appendix to Dr. Watts's Psalms and Hymns*.

19. Proverbs 6:27–29: "Can a man carry fire next to his chest and his clothes and not be burned? Or can one walk on hot coals and his feet not be scorched? So is he who goes in to his neighbor's wife; none who touches her will go unpunished" (ESV).

20. Philippians 1:9–10.

Chapter 8: Whatever Is Lovely

1. Evan Bates, *Japanese Love Poems: Selections from the Manyōshū* (Mineola, NY: Dover Publications, 2005), 53.

2. It has been suggested that one reason women fulfill this role in the community is because women's bodies have more subcutaneous fat than men's,

which helps keep them warm in the cold water. Traditionally, *ama* dove wearing only a loincloth and headscarf. Modern-day *ama* wear wetsuits.

3. The ease with which Paul juxtaposes purity and loveliness (beauty) suggests that our modern notions of both are severely anemic.

4. Elaine Scarry, *On Beauty and Being Just* (Princeton: Princeton University Press, 1999), 30.

5. Psalm 19:1.

6. Gregory Wolfe, "The Wound of Beauty," *Image Journal,* issue 56, accessed March 28, 2018, https://imagejournal.org/article/the-wound-of-beauty/.

7. Revelation 21:21.

8. "Legacy," Mikimoto America, accessed March 29, 2018, https://www.mikimotoamerica.com/legacy.

9. Genesis 1:31. The Hebrew word "good" can also be translated "beautiful," so God saw everything that He had made and behold, it was very good and beautiful and lovely.

10. This is not a statement about children's morality; if you were a helpless being who could not feed, clean, or clothe yourself, you'd be pretty demanding too.

11. Mark A. Noll, *The Scandal of the Evangelical Mind* (Grand Rapids, MI: Eerdmans, 1994), 12.

12. Proverbs 31:30.

13. 1 Timothy 5:1–2.

14. "On the Job with Japan's Legendary Female Ama Divers," CNN, February 23, 2017, https://www.cnn.com/travel/article/japanese-ama-divers/index.html.

15. Bates, *Japanese Love Poems*, 57.

Chapter 9: Whatever Is Commendable

1. We derive our English word "euphemism" from this same root.

2. Matthew Harmon, *Philippians: A Mentor Commentary* (Fearn, UK: Christian Focus Publications, 2015), 422.

3. Quintilian, *Institutio Oratoria*, with an English translation by Harold Edgeworth Butler, (Cambridge, MA: Harvard University Press; London: William Heinemann, Ltd., 1920), http://www.perseus.tufts.edu/hopper/text?doc=Quint.Inst.2.17&lang=original.

4. Annie Dillard, *The Writing Life* (New York: Harper Perennial, 1990), 32.

5. Samuel Butler, "Characters and Passages from Note-Books," 1908, 206, Questia, https://www.questia.com/read/91303857/characters-and-passages-from-note-books.

6. Like you, I wondered what this word meant. Research proved inconclusive although a contemporary scientific text uses it to speak of the weight of a liquid. In Latin, *hali* means breath or air, so my understanding is that *halitious* means that something is of a light or insubstantial nature. The English word halitosis comes from the same root, so I suppose it is also possible that King Charles was concerned with regulating coffee breath. But most likely not.

7. "By the King: A Proclamation for the Suppression of Coffee-houses," 1675, accessed March 27, 2018, https://www.staff.uni-giessen.de/~g909/tx/suppress.htm.

8. Peter Dizikes, "Study: On Twitter, False News Travels Faster than True Stories," *MIT News*, March 8, 2018, http://news.mit.edu/2018/study-twitter-false-news-travels-faster-true-stories-0308.

9. Matthew 12:33–37.

10. Abusers and manipulators often try to use this verse to silence those reporting abuse to relevant authorities. It's also convenient for avoiding the truth about the evil behavior of a person, organization, or country that we love.

11. One of the dangers of legalism is that it gives improper weight to what is important and what is not. At best, it equalizes all issues, making lifestyle choices as significant as clear immorality. At worst, it completely inverts moral teaching, making lifestyle choices more binding than the "more important matters of the law—justice, mercy, and faithfulness." (See Matt. 23:23.)

12. "Nobel Prize Speech," Elie Wiesel Foundation for Humanity, September 26, 2017, http://eliewieselfoundation.org/elie-wiesel/nobelprizespeech/.

13. It's fascinating to watch women wield a similar relational power online, leveraging intimacy and social agility to form powerful communities. From network marketing to the blogosphere, women aren't moving into public spaces so much as expanding the boundaries of their private lives and thus their influence.

14. *Fierce Convictions: The Extraordinary Life of Hannah More: Poet, Reformer, Abolitionist* by Karen Swallow Prior is an interesting biography of one such woman.

15. Sources attribute the poem to the poet and hymnist William Cowper. It can be found online and in anthologies of Cowper's work.

16. Isaiah 52:7.

Chapter 10: Every Good Gift

1. Proverbs 16:9 and 16:33 show "A person's heart plans his way, but the LORD determines his steps" and "The lot is cast into the lap, but its every decision is from the LORD." Whether by planning or chance, all comes from Him.

2. Joseph Brodsky, "How to Read a Book," *The New York Times,* June 12, 1988, https://www.nytimes.com/1988/06/12/books/how-to-read-a-book.html.

3. The skill of putting a book down is one every reader should master. You do not owe the author a reading. It is the author's job to write in a way that draws you in and keeps you engaged. If this book does not keep your attention, I now extend my unqualified permission to close it and go read something else.

4. Some scholars have labeled the book of James as the "Proverbs of the New Testament," noting its emphasis on wisdom and practical application.

5. Matthew 13:24–30.

6. Exodus 23:8; Proverbs 19:6.

7. Luke 16:1–13.

8. Romans 14:23.

9. Romans 2:4. I am not suggesting license that presumes on the goodness of God but a faith that knows Him to be kind and good.

10. James Montgomery Boice, *Philippians: An Expositional Commentary* (Grand Rapids, MI: Zondervan, 1971), 283–84.

11. "Quotable Quotes," ECFA website, http://www.ecfa.org/trust/Quotable Quotes.aspx.

12. *Look and See: A Portrait of Wendell Berry*, directed by Laura Dunn, USA: Two Birds Film, 2017, Netflix.

13. According to the conscious competence model of learning a new skill, we begin by not knowing we lack a skill (unconscious incompetence) to knowing we lack it (conscious incompetence) to actively trying to develop it (conscious competence) to finally, practicing it without thinking (unconscious competence).

Chapter 11: Our Common Good

1. Alan Jacobs, *How to Think: A Survival Guide for a World at Odds* (New York: Currency, 2017), 37.

2. Proverbs 13:20. It is not always possible to completely extricate ourselves from proximity to foolish people, but when we can't, we must take precaution to identify them as such—if only mentally—and in so far as possible, avoid depending on them or following their counsel.

3. In 1 Corinthians 11:1, Paul issues a similar call when he says "Be imitators of me, as I am of Christ" (ESV).
4. Romans 14:4, 6, 10–11.
5. Romans 14:23 warns believers of the danger of ignoring their conscience in order to participate in activities that they are sensitive to, saying, "Whatever does not proceed from faith is sin" (ESV).
6. In a parallel passage in 1 Corinthians 8:13, Paul writes: "Therefore, if food causes my brother or sister to fall, I will never again eat meat, so that I won't cause my brother or sister to fall."
7. Romans 14:7, 15, 20.
8. 1 Corinthians 10:31–33.
9. Jacobs, *How to Think*, 59.
10. Nouwen, Laird, and Christensen, *Discernment: Reading the Signs of Daily Life*, 23.
11. In Romans 9:19–21, Paul notes that none of us are in a position to question how and why God formed us the way He has. He is speaking in context of redemption, but the principle is larger than this specific application.
12. Massimo Montanari, *Food Is Culture* (New York: Columbia University Press, 2006), 94.
13. 1 Corinthians 11:23–26.
14. John 6:48–58.

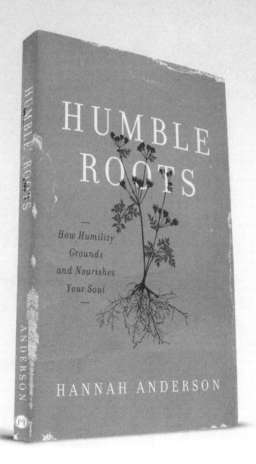

Do you long to live the life he created for you?

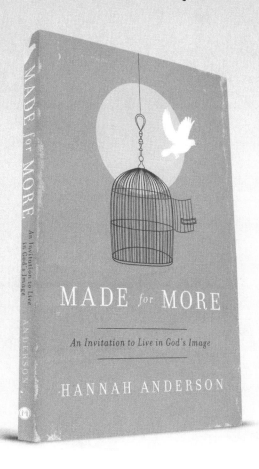